IOWA
TRANSLATIONS

PAUL ENGLE

GENERAL EDITOR

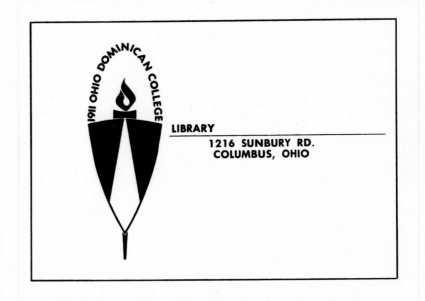

MODERN CHINESE POETRY

TWENTY POETS
FROM THE
REPUBLIC OF CHINA
1955-1965

SELECTED AND TRANSLATED BY

WAI-LIM YIP

UNIVERSITY OF IOWA PRESS ѱ IOWA CITY

895.1
Y51m
1970

Library of Congress Catalog Card Number: 78–118721
University of Iowa Press, Iowa City 52240
© 1970 by The University of Iowa. All rights reserved
Printed in the United States of America
Designed by John B. Goetz
ISBN 87745-004-8

FOR
MY WIFE TZU-MEI
MY DAUGHTER CHEN
AND MY SON CHO

Foreword

Theology once believed that "translation" could mean direct removal to heaven of the body without intervening death. All too often in being translated, the poem loses its life.

Literal translation of a poem into bare prose may help understanding, but the plain text of a literal version may not be accurate to the poem, for what a poet writes is not a literal account of his life, but an imaginative vision of it. Only a translator with imagination can truly translate the imaginative language of a poem.

The Iowa Translations series brings together people of creative talent with those expert in a language. We believe that in the hazardous twentieth century men of good mind and good will must talk to each other or die. We believe that poetry is the highest form of talk, and that translating it is therefore an honor and a privilege as well as one of the toughest jobs known to man.

Wai-lim Yip brings to these translations a firm poetic gift, as his own poems prove. His selections of recent Chinese verse dramatize an astonishing continuity of ancient tradition with a shrewd use of contemporary images, details and idioms. They prove that all of us, in whatever culture, endure this world in common. When Ching-lin Wang of today's Taipei cries, "How much truth can a blade of grass bear," he is less a poet from a foreign country than Whitman's neighbor in Camden. These poems illuminate us because they bring Chinese light to our day.

PAUL ENGLE, General Editor
Director, International Writing Program
School of Letters, The University of Iowa

Preface

Driven by an almost superstitious fear that much of the poetry included in this anthology would be obliterated by the avalanche of world crises very much the way a few significant Chinese poets of the forties and the fifties had been buried by untimely eventfulness, I began some of these translations as early as 1962 in Taipei in the hope that these recast artifacts would perhaps have a chance to survive.

The same year, a grant from Paul Engle, then Director of the Program in Creative Writing at The University of Iowa, and the Asia Foundation brought me to Iowa City where I had an excellent opportunity to continue working on these translations while writing my own poetry. To them I am particularly grateful. Special acknowledgment is also made to The JDR 3rd Fund (Porter A. McCray, director), The Louis W. and Maud Hill Family Foundation of St. Paul (A. A. Heckman, executive director), the Iowa Electric Light and Power Company (the late Sutherland Dows), the John Deere Company (William Hewitt, chairman), the Maytag Company of Newton, Iowa, the *Reader's Digest* (DeWitt Wallace, chairman), *Life* magazine, the *Des Moines Register* and *Tribune*, and Gardner Cowles (New York), Mrs. Marshall Field (New York), and others, all of whom gave funds which helped make this book possible. In a practical world, they cared about the imagination.

The poets chosen here are essentially those who had achieved their own identity between the years 1955 and 1965, although some of the poems in this book were actually written after 1965. Almost all the poets are from Taiwan; seven of them from the army or the navy. Poets who emerge as significant voices after 1965 are not included; the translator has to set himself a working span of time. Most of these poems appeared principally in the following magazines: *Ch'uang-shih-chi* (*The Epoch Poetry Quarterly*), eds. Chang Mo, Lo Fu, and Ya Hsien; *Hsien-tai-shih* (*Modern Poetry*), ed. Chi Hsien; *Lan-hsing-shih-yeh* (*Blue Stars Poetry Leaf*), ed. Yü Kwang-chung; *Lan-hsing chi-k'an* (*Blue Stars Quarterly*), ed. Ch'in Tzu-hao and others; *Wen-hsüeh tsa-chih* (*Literary Review*), ed. Hsia Tsi-an; *Hsien-tai wen-hsüeh* (*Modern Literature Quarterly*), eds. Pai Hsien-yung and Wang Wen-hsin; and *Modern Literature and Arts Association* publications, ed. Quanam Shum (Hong Kong).

In the preparation of this anthology, several poets and friends had assisted in various ways and to them I would like to acknowledge my debts: Donald Justice and Mark Strand, both distinguished poets, spent many hours with me going over the style of some of the poems. Edmund Keeley of Princeton University, stimulating teacher and friend, also read part of the manuscript during his brief stay in Iowa. James Boyer May and Milton VanSickle, editors of *Trace* which published a portion of this book in its No. 54 issue, have given me continual moral support. Wang Ching-hsien (Yeh Shan), one of the poets in this book, has provided me with materials not available in this country. All the poets have been cooperative in providing me with special biographical details and calligraphic signatures. The poets' names in this collection are arranged with the pen name given first and the real name in parentheses.

A few of these poems appeared in the *Texas Quarterly* (Spring 1967).

My wife Tzu-mei, under great stress in these years of foreign residence, typed almost the entire manuscript and to her especially I want to dedicate this book.

Wai-lim Yip
University of California, San Diego

Introduction

The *Pai-hua* and Modern Chinese Poetry

First, a definition of the *pai-hua*. The *pai-hua* is the written colloquial language adopted by Chinese writers after the May Fourth Movement in 1919 to replace the literary or classical Chinese, *wen-yen,* as the primary means of literary expression. While the colloquial expressions of the *pai-hua* have many differences from those of the literary Chinese, they have been further modified by Occidental grammatical structures in the process of introducing and translating Western literatures into China in the past six decades. In order to give a clear perspective of the nature of the written colloquial language as a poetic medium without mulling over all the historical elements involved, I propose to compare it with that of the literary Chinese in the example of a Li Po poem. Using it as a means of contrast and/or comparison, I will try to bring into the foreground the limitations as well as new possibilities of the *pai-hua* before discussing some of the ways in which the modern Chinese poets exploit the medium.

Now then, let me lay out the Li Po poem in the most literal way possible, giving first the original (arranged horizontally from left to right for the sake of convenience); second, a word-for-word translation; third, an approximation almost as literal but with a few additions (those in brackets) introduced to make it English.

1)

1. 青 山 橫 北 郭
2. 白 水 繞 東 城

3. 此　地　一　為　別

4. 孤　蓬　萬　里　征

5. 浮　雲　遊　子　意

6. 落　日　故　人　情

7. 揮　手　自　茲　去

8. 蕭　蕭　班　馬　鳴

2)
1. green	mountain[s]	lie-across	north	outer-wall-of-city
2. white	water	wind-around	east	city
3. this	place	once	make	separation
4. lone	tumbleweed	ten-thousand	mile[s]	travel
5. floating	cloud[s]	wanderer		thought (mood)
6. setting	sun	old	friend	feeling
7. wave	hand[s]	from	here	go
8. *hsiao*	*hsiao**	parting	horse	neigh

* onomatopoeic words for neighing.

3) 1. Green mountain[s] lie across [the] north wall.
   2. White water wind[s] [the] east city.
   3. Here once [we] part.
   4. Lone tumbleweed [;] [a] million mile[s] [to] travel.
   5. Floating cloud[s] [;] [a] wanderer['s] mood.
   6. Setting sun [;] [an] old friend['s] feeling.
   7. [We] wave hand[s,] [you] go from here.
   8. Neigh, neigh goes [the] horse at parting.

Presently, I will discuss this poem's unique presentation in several ways, but let me first point out a few peculiarities (i.e., judging them against English) and then I will have occasion to return to the syntactical aspects:

(1) Except in rare cases, there is practically no enjambment in Chinese poetry; each line is a complete unit of meaning.

(2) Typical of most Chinese poems, this poem is free from the restriction of the personal pronoun (the use of which tends to specify the speaker

or protagonist), hence making it possible to have an *impersonal* speaker for a *universal* situation although it may have meant to portray a personal experience. This non-commitment to a specified agent, strengthened by the fact that Chinese verbs have no declensions, is to return to "pure actions" and "pure states of being." The insertion of "we" and "you" in the approximation is required by English but not by Chinese.

(3) Similarly, the classical Chinese allows the poets to avoid committing actions or states of being to finite time. The *tense*less nature of the Chinese verbs makes this peculiarly interesting. The so-called past, present, and future tenses in Indo-European languages are means to set time and space limits even on the linguistic level. The Chinese verbs *tend* to return to Phenomenon itself *which is timeless, the concept of time being a human invention imposed upon Phenomenon.* (By *Phenomenon,* I mean particularly the Taoist "totality of the spontaneity of all forms of existence.") Only in rare cases would the Chinese poets use elements like "today," "tomorrow," and "yesterday" to indicate finite time, and they always use them for special effects. But even then, the verbs remain unchanged, for there is no conjugation of this kind in the Chinese sentence.

With these preliminary explanations, we are ready to examine the syntactical structures of the lines. The structure of each line can be understood in terms of the combinations of characters by which meaning patterns are formed. A common structure is the first two lines which may be represented, numerically, as 2-1-2, where the middle character is usually a connective (verb, preposition, or adjective which assumes the character of a verb) serving to tighten the relation between the units before or after it. This structure most resembles the English subject-verb-object relation, making it unusually felicitous to translate into English. But let me use two versions which deviate from this simple structure to show, by contrary evidence, the special mode of presentation in the classical Chinese poem.[1]

> Where blue hills cross the northern sky,
> Beyond the moat which girds the town,
> 'Twas there we stopped to say Goodbye!
>
> > Giles

> With a blue line of mountains north of the wall,
> And east of the city a white curve of water,
> Here you must leave me and drift away . . .
>
> > Bynner

[1] For a fuller treatment of the problems of translating the classical Chinese poem, see my *Ezra Pound's Cathay* (Princeton, 1969), pp. 8–33, or *DELOS*/3 (Austin, Texas, 1969), pp. 62–79.

In the original, and even in the approximation of the original, we see things in nature working upon us, while in Giles and Bynner, we are *led* to these things by way of intellectual, directive devices ("where" and "with," etc.). We see the process of analysis at work rather than the things acting themselves out before us. In the original, it is as if the poet has become *a spotlight showing the states of being to us* where in Giles and Bynner (i.e., with the addition of intellectual directives), we have *a narrator explaining things to us.* This is an important difference. The cinematic effect of the classical Chinese poem is even sharper in the next type of structure—which may be represented numerically, as 2–3. Lines 5 and 6 of the above poem belong to this category. But for the sake of clarification, a line from Tu Fu is instructive here:

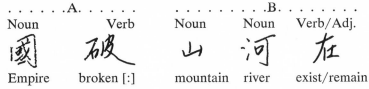

. . . . . .A. . . . . .　　. . . . . .B. . . . .
Noun　　　Verb　　Noun　　Noun　　Verb/Adj.

Empire　　broken [:]　　mountain　river　　exist/remain

This line has been translated as:

> Though a country be sundered, hills and rivers endure.
> > Bynner (1929)
> A nation though fallen, the land yet remains.
> > W. J. B. Fletcher (1933)
> The state may fall, but the hills and streams remain.
> > David Hawkes (1967)

Note how such analytical or explanatory elements as "though," "yet," or "but" have destroyed the montage presentation in the original (which the paratactical nature of the Chinese line enforces), characterized by the simultaneous presences of the "broken empire" and "mountains and rivers." Two phases of perception, like two cones of light, cut into each other simultaneously. The reader, following the spotlight, feels, by himself, *without being told,* the contrast and tension in the scenery so presented. Similarly, in lines 5 and 6 of the Li Po poem, one may first ask this question: Does line 5 mean, syntactically, "floating clouds *are* a wanderer's mood" (i.e., "a wanderer's mood *is* floating clouds"), or "floating clouds *are like* a wanderer's mood" (i.e., "a wanderer's mood *is like* floating clouds")? The answer is: it does and it does not at the same time. No one would fail to perceive the resemblance of a wanderer's drifting life (and the mood it creates) to the floating clouds. But there is a flash of interest in the syntactically uncommitted resemblance which the introduction of "is" or "are" and "is like" or "are like" destroys. In this case, we actually see the floating clouds and the wanderer (and the state of mind he is in) simultaneously. This simultaneous presence of two objects, like the juxtaposition of two separate shots, "resembles not so much a simple sum of one shot plus another shot—as it does a *creation*. It resembles a creation—rather than a sum of its parts—from the circumstance that in every such juxtaposition *the result is qualitatively* distinguishable from each component element viewed separately." [2]

Indeed, what makes most of these short classical Chinese poems so uniquely rich and yet simple is this cinematic presentation of pure actions or states of being without the interference of any intellectual fumbling. In a line like Li Po's

> Phoenix gone, terrace empty, river flows on alone.
> (Shot 1)   (Shot 2)   (Shot 3)

do we need any more words to explain the vicissitude of time versus the permanence of Nature?

By now we can see that the other characteristics of the literary Chinese are conducive to this cinematic presentation which emphasizes phases of perception through spotlighting activities rather than through analysis. The making of shots (phases of perception) *tend* to demand conciseness and shorter lines, hence no enjambment. Longer lines easily stretch into explanation. The priority given to the direct confrontation between the actions or states of being and the audience, and to audience participation, obliterates the consciousness of time (i.e., the mechanical divisions of time). This directness is enhanced by the *tense*less nature of the Chinese verbs. The freedom from the intrusion of the personal pronoun, as I have explained earlier, universalizes the situation, enabling the poet to have an objective (but not discursive) presentation of a subjective experience.

Turning from the potentialities of the literary Chinese as a poetic medium to the written colloquial (*pai-hua*), one is struck by some marked differences: (1) Although the new medium is flexible enough to yield lines that would be free from the restriction of the personal pronoun, many Chinese poets *tend* to bring it into the poem. (2) Like the literary Chinese, the new medium is equally *tense*less, but more time-indicators have been

allowed into the making of a poem. Some examples are *ts'eng* 曾, *i-ching* 巳經 , and *kuo* 過 to indicate past time, *chiang* 將 to indicate

---

[2] Sergei M. Eisenstein, *The Film Sense* (New York, 1924), p. 7.

future, and *cho* 着 to indicate progressive.[3] (3) There are many enjamb-
ments in modern Chinese poetry. (4) Whereas the paratactical lines in
classical Chinese poetry achieve a dramatic quality similar to the spotlight-
ing activity, the users of the new medium have, consciously or uncon-
sciously, ushered in analytical elements, very much the way one of the
translators did to the Tu Fu line quoted above when he rendered it into
the *pai-hua*:

國　　破　　山　　河　　在

empire　　broken　　mountain[s]　　river[s]　　exist

becomes, in Liu Ta-ch'eng's hand [15 characters to the original 5],

國家/已經/破碎了/祇是/山河/依然/如故

country (empire)/already/broken/only/mountain river/still/
as before.[4]

"Already" (*i-ching*) indicates past and "only" and "still" are analytical
elements destroying both the montage presentation and the directness in the
same manner the English versions have turned drama into analysis. Lines
of this kind, to our surprise, abound in much of the poetry written in the
new medium. An early example, for instance, is from Liu Ta-pai (1880–
1932) which runs, in Kai-yu Hsu's translation:

> My brother's wife weaves cloth,
> My brother sells it.
> But there is no cloth
> To mend my worn pants.
> > *Twentieth Century Chinese Poetry*, p. xxii.

[3] It should be pointed out, however, that many of these indicators exist in classical
Chinese prose (and in the novels which are largely written in the colloquial). But
since the function of the prose is more or less analytical and the structure of the novel
linear, these indicators are appropriate. (We can see why the modern novel, deadly
opposed to analytical and linear structures, has to destroy the temporal order to
achieve its end.) Some of these indicators do appear in classical Chinese poetry, but
not as frequently and seldom as structural pegs.

[4] Two characters in the *pai-hua* (and sometimes more than two) tend to make a
compound. I put slashes to indicate them for the sake of a close corresponding word-
for-word annotation. Most of the modern Chinese poets would think that such a line
should not be translated at all. The example is used here merely to expose the unhappy
tendencies of the new medium.

A recent example can be found, almost at random, in Yü Kuang-chung:

> In May this year, everything is still the same as before.
> Brightness still exists, but the soul of fire is dead.
>
> "Stalactite"

But, in a sense, none of these poets is to blame; it seems the *pai-hua* as a poetic medium entails these weaknesses that tend to grip hold of its users. (I repeatedly use the word *tendency,* because these weaknesses can be easily overcome since the new medium, if manipulated suitably—as some of us have done—can give the same performance as the literary Chinese without incurring any distortion of the language.)

The analytical tendency of the *pai-hua* is perhaps the result of several factors. First, inherent discursiveness. Before the poets adopted the *pai-hua* as a medium, it had been exploited largely by the novelists; all the poems found in the novels were written in classical Chinese and when a moment of poetic intensity arose, the novelists would turn to classical Chinese lines of poetry for assistance rather than trying to make the colloquial poetic. And the novel, being a linear structure, emphasizes logical developments and causal relations and operates with many analytical elements. When the poets adopted the medium, all the discursiveness came with it. Although we consider it necessary to use the colloquial instead of the literary Chinese, which has by now become stilted and incapable of authenticating contemporary feeling, we can accuse many of our predecessors of having done too little to refine the new medium by getting rid of this discursiveness. The situation is worsened by the intrusion of Western sciences, systems of logic, and forms of poetry. The *pai-hua* is being Europeanized (as the Chinese called it) in the process of translation (both journalistic and literary). Many efforts have been made to fit the Procrustean bed: introduction of Occidental syntax, adoption of foreign grammatical frameworks as bases for the Chinese sentence, and application of punctuation to regulate and clarify Chinese linguistic structures. All these were intended, no doubt, to tell the world that we have just as much logic and are just as scientific as the West, as if poetic ambiguity and richness were a shame!

With a medium so deviated from the literary Chinese, to what extent can the modern Chinese poets, now obviously working against odds, still retain their identity with the classical Chinese poetic mode? But there is further complication in the problem that we have to take up first. Not only have the linguistic features been changed, their aesthetic perception also has shifted emphases.

Ironically enough, many early *pai-hua* poets, attackers of Confucianism for its Procrustean methods, should be writing poetry in a discursive manner, which is farthest away from the classical Chinese mode (the implied poetics of which derived from Chuangtzu who also criticized Confucius in similar terms). With the translation and imitation of the romantics and the symbolists in the thirties and the forties,[5] our poets began to remove some of the obvious prosaic elements for more imagery. By this time, the relation between the actions portrayed and the agent of the actions as well as the poet's attempt to relate himself to the objects around him began to stay put in the *pai-hua* poetry, although, lacking the mystical zeal of the romantics and the symbolists, they had not produced any genuine romantic or symbolist poetry.

The poets represented in this anthology, following on the heels of this mode, working with the odds of the *pai-hua* (and new possibilities afforded by Western poetry which I will bring up later), and after some false starts, are found advocating even greater ellipticity. One will notice, for instance, further elimination of connecting links, a greater degree of merging with the objects, less reliance on the linear structure, more psychological links than linguistic links (no doubt spurred partly by the Surrealists), and greater effort to refine the *pai-hua* by readmitting many literary Chinese phrases for conciseness. But as yet, there is no rejection of the romantic and symbolist influence; in fact, they are initially enchanted by it and, in particular, by the metaphysical unrest of the post-symbolists:

> In today's society, science has brought us into a new dinosaur age. Human life is being forced into a chain of endless mechanical movements. Under the oppression of this urban civilization, Poetry has become almost the only sign of human existence.
>
> . . . .
>
> In one single poem, I am constantly trying to get into it what it is not usually expected to contain, so that it can comprehend all the complexities in human existence, from the Ultimate to love, death, spiritual quests, disillusions, fear, anxiety, hollowness and despair—in one sentence, I want to gulp down all the complex variegation in one's sensibility—I become so covetous that I can hardly get at a focus.
>
> Ya Hsien, "The Poet's Notebook"

Or witness this prose-poem by Shang Ch'in:

[5] For a brief history of the development of the poetry in those years, read the "Introduction" to Kai-yu Hsu's *Twentieth Century Chinese Poetry* (New York, 1963).

"We should turn off the light before undressing, otherwise LIGHT will stay on our flesh."

"Because of its hold on you?"

"Because of its being an insulator."

"What about the moon then?"

"Even the stars are the same." After the light is turned off, the curtain falls down; outside the window is nothing but the stiff night. Inside the house a person, after having lost his hair, has lost also his lips and tongue; the arms each from its back and shoulder, from the breasts and waist, disappear; his legs and his ankles go a little bit later. After that, what is left is the so-called BEING.

N'ETRE PAS [sic]. They were not being dissolved by darkness; they took part in and purified DARKNESS and thus: Alas, how difficult it is to make a black crystal of no substance.

"The Black Crystal of No Substance"

While the doubtlessly magnificent presentation of the classical Chinese poem persists as an ideal toward which we should work continuously, it has its limitations. It is a poetry of the Phenomenon *in one instant's epiphany* and usually *in a static equilibrium* made possible by the bird's-eye view spotlighting. As such, it cannot embrace an encyclopaedic vision of many moments of reality arrested in their dynamic ordering. The detachment (enforced by the presentational uniqueness, although the merging of the poet with the objects is assumed) has also ruled out any type of the feverish inner debate of a Hamlet or of an agonized Macbeth, with which modern Chinese poets are deeply obsessed, crushed as they are by the traumatic breakup of the Chinese world-view, and a nightmarish, mutilated reality, as well as by the fearful existential absurdity around them.

Of course, the question ready to be asked is: between these obsessions and the classical poetic mode, what have modern Chinese poets offered to the world that they can claim to be uniquely their own? Also, what are some of the means by which they exorcise the evil spirits in the medium so that it can return closer to Phenomenon itself? Some of the characteristics enumerated above, namely elimination of links of connection, merging with the objects, anti-linear structures, etc., in these poets are not, as we shall see, the result of deliberate dislocation of the language, as in Pound and others, because the *pai-hua,* even with the intrusion of analytical elements, still contains many of the potentialities of the classical Chinese (e.g., the *tense*less nature) and can be refined through the filter of good poetry without violating the natural flow of the language. The very first step toward this refinement is to grasp hold of a self-contained image or phase of perception as it emerges from Phenomenon. A self-contained image may be defined as one capable of giving forth a poetic vigor without the rest of the context. A good self-contained image or phase of perception can, in fact, be considered a poem in itself. It is sufficient in this sense because it carries the force of the entire situation, as, for example, these lines:

> At the end of my shadow there sits a woman, weeping.
>
> Ya Hsien, "Abyss"
>
> How deep and how blue is the melancholy to starboard!
>
> Shang Ch'in, "The Captain"
>
> O to stride outside, one mere step is nostalgia.
>
> Cheng Ch'ou-yü, "Border Tavern"
>
> Are the two kites flying two children or the two children
>   flying two kites?
>
> Kuan Kuan, "Spring Song"

In the last example is found another aspect that is closely related to the making of a self-contained image or phase of perception. This is the trance-like mode of consciousness with which the poet perceives the world. In this consciousness, limits of space and time do not exist and, because of this fact, the poet can free the moment from its larger context as well as from the linear, causal developments that go either before or after it, and hence allows it to achieve a visual distinctiveness similar to the spotlighting effect of the classical Chinese line. In this consciousness, I once remarked, the poet has "another hearing, another vision. He hears voices we normally do not hear. He sees activities across a space not to be seen by the physical eye." Indeed, all true lyric poets start from this trance-like consciousness. Thus, Shang Ch'in:

> Skirts burnt by our gaze, pretty bodies
> Dissolve in a lane of sunshine
> Leaving the gradient of the Milky Way
> In the empty drinking glass.

In this mystical act of losing oneself in objects or moments is found a singular mode of aesthetic perception. Another stanza from Shang Ch'in's "Gradient of the Milky Way" is illuminating:

> The Milky Way lowers itself to the water.
> Stars cry out silently.
> Many simple limbs and forms
> Are moved by their own shadows.

The guitar sails on the sound-wave and
                              the meadow
Drifts under the cordage;
Sheds tears
              and becomes the sister of the pond.
Between the high-tension wire and the grape trellis
The Milky Way stoops toward itself,

That is, straight toward my southeast.
The dead sound of the motor is bound
By two lines of eucalyptus.
                              The mildewed
Sighing becomes a sound-blast at midnight.

Here we have a lyricism in which the poet, merged with the objects, allows their inner lives to grow, change and gesticulate by themselves according to their own natural laws, and yet maintains a certain amount of his subjectivity. But in relating to Phenomenon, he does not impose his subjective self upon the order that is shaping itself from this cosmic scheme; rather he considers his subjective self part of Phenomenon participating in the shaping.

Similarly, Cheng Ch'ou-yü and Yeh Shan place themselves in a synchronous relation with the circulation of stars or with mountains and flowers:

Meteorites strike on our shoulders of coarse linen.
Water gurgles from the native town of stars.
And mountains, bud-like, lock the flowers
Under our bare feet,
Unable to go farther ahead, ahead being sky's end.
                              Cheng Ch'ou-yü, "The Mount of
                              Might: Impressions"

Diggers rest beneath trees.
Tree shadows slowly slant eastward.
Searchers of butterfly-orchids are clambering
A snow-white precipice. Forests in the distance
Look as if growing in a previous century.
Small birds clamor, like a waterfall
A waterfall without any sense of seasons.
                              Yeh Shan, "Strawberry Fields in Summer"

An annotation to these passages is a stanza from one of Yeh Shan's early poems, "News":

On the way home, many bird corpses,
Many round eyes, bulging and smiling;
Some gunmen are wiping sweat in the teahouse,
Looking at the scenery . . . .

To modern Chinese poets, poetry should be the approximation of the fluctuations of Phenomenon, not its anatomy.

It is clear from these examples that the approximation of the fluctuations of Phenomenon owes much, in Shang Ch'in, Cheng Ch'ou-yü and Yeh Shan to the distinctiveness given to each phase of perception. Indeed, with distinctiveness, in the kind that is found in Li Po's "Phoenix gone (Shot one), terrace empty (Shot two), river flows on alone (Shot 3)," [6] no discursiveness would get in the way. In the same vein, Ya Hsien allows, in his poem "Salt," the distinctiveness of his images to *act out* the irony in the fate of an old woman:

Our old woman had never met Dostoevsky after all. In the spring
she only cried: Salt! Give me a peck of salt! The angels were
singing in the elms. That year the garden peas scarcely blossomed.

Seven hundred miles away the camel caravans led by the Minister of
Salt were passing along the seaside. No blade of seaweed ever
showed up in our old woman's pupils. She only cried: Salt!
Salt! Give me a peck of salt! The laughing angels covered her
up with a shower of snow.

In 1911 the partymen arrived in Wu-chang. Our old woman left her
foot-binding cloth up on the elms and went off into the breath
of wild dogs and under the wings of the bald-headed vulture.
Many voices whined in the winds: Salt! Salt! Give me a peck
of salt! Almost all the garden peas blossomed with white flowers
that year. After all Dostoevsky had never met our old Woman.

A simple "but" between "Give me a peck of salt!" and "The laughing angels covered her up with a shower of snow" would turn the whole poem into prose.

One may notice that although the poet has used a narrative procedure here, one is not bothered by it. This is so because the poet has turned the procedure into a pseudo-discursiveness mainly to satisfy the reader's mental habits, just as Shang Ch'in sometimes uses pseudo-syntax to negate syntax.

[6] The most inexcusable distortion of this line is in Witter Bynner's translation (with the collaboration of a classical Chinese scholar!) which runs: Phoenixes that played here once, so that the place was named for them/*Have abandoned it now to this desolate river*. If this is poetry, what else isn't?

The deadman's face is a swamp unseen by men;
A swamp in the wasteland is the escape of part of the sky.
The fugitive sky is the brimming of roses;
The brimming of roses is the snow that has never fallen.
The fallen snow is a string being twanged;
A string being twanged is a tear in the veins.
The rising tears are burning hearts;
Burnt hearts are swamps, their wastelands.

"The Escaping Sky"

The "is" does not function metaphorically here, as it normally does. What we have here is one image superimposed upon another image until it comes back almost full circle. This is like the movie projector casting one shot after another in quick succession. But the poem here is richer. While playing upon the reader's mental habits, it starts the reader on one line of thinking, i.e., searching for resemblance (which is no doubt also there), but a new line of thinking starts after reading about three verses, i.e., the reader begins to feel the impact of superimposition. The two lines of thinking form a tension and yet, at the same time, one complements the other.

The pseudo-syntax is but one form of revenge against the analytical tendency of the *pai-hua*. Along with this manipulation is the attempt to play down the significance of the personal pronoun, as, for instance, the "I" in the "Gradient of the Milky Way" is subordinate to the shaping force of the cosmic scheme. So are certain aspects of the technological reality, such as "sound-waves," "high-tension wire," and "motor" in that poem.

But what about the nightmarish, mutilated reality in the midst of demolishing war, rapid industrialization and commercialism, and the violent and fearful existential absurdity which modern poets, especially Ya Hsien and Lo Fu, "covet" so much? How can poets still provide an equilibrium for these chaotic, savagely anomalous aspects of reality in contemporary history? This is indeed a great challenge. In the words of Ya Hsien: "I want to gulp down all the complex variegation in one's sensibility—I become so covetous that I can hardly get at a focus."

For the Chinese, some details from contemporary experience are jarring in the midst of natural elements, as in this example by Kuan Kuan:

> In the forest
> Fruits and fruits clamor noisily, nagging the wind, complaining
> that he should not, really should not have cut their slips into such
> a beautiful confusion and let pass the shoes of a young man
> whose collars are turned up,
> And who is at the same time smoking.

"A Stopover Visitor"

However, to ignore these anomalous experiences is to sin. It is the poet's task, a mission almost, to effect a poetry giving form and expression to the drastic change in feeling, destiny, and life, mixed with anxiety and solitude, nostalgia and expectancy, exile (metaphysical and physical) and dreams, fear and doubt in contemporary China, in spite of the lack of what David Jones called "a civilizational situation." [7] The challenge has yielded distinctively variegated results in modern Chinese poetry.

Kuan Kuan, probably inspired by the neuroticism of a poem by Shang Ch'in (written before Kafkaesque neuroticism was known to China) which is about a cab driver weeping over an illusion that he had actually crashed into himself while still in the driver's seat of his own cab, transforms ragged and vicious experiences, mixed with a nostalgia tempered by the playful seriousness of children, into the vision of a sensitive and chimerical man:

> . . . The man who had just taken over the sentry saw with his own eyes the evening's red-embroidered shoes being stolen and the sea's skirt torn to pieces by bitches.—O what a strange man!—he did not even fire his rifle at them or report this to the lieutenant, but became absorbed in the beauty of a wild chrysanthemum he planted in his barrel and insisted that it was a woman; and then, he hummed a happy tune: *Little mother, I am brave and brassy.*

> > 'Signal fires continue for three long months;
> > A letter from home is worth a thousand pieces of gold.'

> But he did not know that without shoes, evening could not return home, that the sea lay on the beach among torn pieces of skirt, weeping. A bitch was mouthing a flare bomb she believed to be a fallen sun; he ought to have believed it, too. But this man, ugh! I simply cannot bear the sight of him.

> A shot from the gun gave the night eyes to see. Meanwhile the night was herding a gang of mice and the moon was herding a school of flying fish. This man grasped a handful of fireflies and rubbed his face with them, saying that his face was hung with stars. He held up his rifle and desperately shot at the stars. Because the mice had eaten away the stock of his rifle? Or maybe because the Hunter had come down to steal his rabbit and had eaten it up and had drunk his *kao-liang?* But the lieutenant said these were no reasons. It was simply that the lieutenant disliked

---

[7] David Jones, *Epoch and Artist*, "If and Perhaps and But" (Chilmark Press: New York, 1963).

the sight of him. The next day he would go to buy a ticket and drink wine.

"The Man Who Rubbed His Face
With Fireflies"

Perhaps one can claim that the shaping force of a cosmic scheme is still at work here since all the objects in this poem are hylozoic. But if it should be called the shaping force of a cosmic scheme, it differs significantly from the harmony, equilibrium, affirmativeness, and calm that are found in the traditional concept. Instead, we have a "fearful," and to the poet a "beautiful," truth. (See Kuan Kuan's statement preceding his poetry in this volume.) And we have a nature modified and extended to include unrest, agony, brutality, irrationality and disorder. As Lo Fu says in his prose statements: "What we see in the mirror is not the image of modern men, but their merciless destinies against which writing poetry is a form of revenge. That is why the language of my poetry often enrages the gods and makes people aware of the stark fact that to live is to stand in the flow of blood." Hence, we see Ya Hsien and Lo Fu, each in his own way, seize upon the *angular tension* and *disjunctive rhythm* of contemporary experiences:

. . . In March I hear the hawking of the cherry.
With the shaking of many tongues spring declines; the bottle flies
    are biting her face:
The slits of the *ch'i-p'ao* swing between certain legs: longing to be read
And entered and worked. And except for death and this
There is nothing definite. Being is wind; being is the noise of the
    thrasher;
Being is—to those who like to be tickled—
To pour out the whole summer of desire.

At night everywhere beds are falling. The sound of a beam of fever-stricken
Light walking on shreds of glass. The forced, blind disorder of
    farming tools.
The scandalous translation of flesh. A terrifying language
Spelled out in kisses. The first acquaintance of blood and blood,
    a flame, a fatigue!
The gesture of ferociously pushing her away.
At night, in Naples, everywhere beds are falling.

At the end of my shadow there sits a woman, weeping.
The baby is interred between snakeroot and tiger lily . . .
The next day we go together to look at the clouds, smile and drink
    plum juice
And dance and dance the last of our manhood away in the dance hall.
. . . .

In the shoulderless city, your book will be pounded into paper pulp
    on the third day.
You wash your face with the night; you duel with your shadow;
You come out from the house and go in and rub your hands . . . .
Ya Hsien, "Abyss"

Merely lifting my head toward a neighboring lane, I am stupefied
In a morning rainbow, walking with a serpent's gait.
Dark hair does not tangle in the blood,
As one, with incompleteness, with long gloom,
Holding a black tributary.

My face spreads like clouds, and thus, the bitter pear tree.
The two pupils move behind the eyes,
Toward directions people dare not talk about:
I am a sawed-off bitter pear tree
On whose annual rings you can still hear clearly winds and cicadas.
. . . .

And so you divide the feast of your own body in the dugouts,
Like doctors who write their theses with plasma exchanging reputations
    for eyeballs,
When guests leave the session one by one,
There will be no more discussion why the sun doesn't come out from the
    gun barrel
So as to let war write biographies for generals.
. . . .

And morning is a beetle that walks on its back,
Chewing as it goes on. I am the leftover night,
Barely hearing stars crying among the joints of teeth.
I write my dying commands on the wind and on the sun about to rise,
And only by sneezing can I remember what eats me is myself.
. . . .

Like a great serpent sloughing off its skin
The city of Spring scatters bloodstained scales.
You come around to see, then complain: that the street's surface is not
    bright enough,
Tempting me to scoop out one of my eyes to supplement it.
O God! What I can offer before your feet is but this much anger.
Lo Fu, "Death in the Stone Cell"

Thus, Ya Hsien and Lo Fu seek to beat life and rhythm into each *fragment*
of experiences, actions, and situations and *let these energized fragments*

work out their own scheme. What we have here is a poetry again of pseudo-discursiveness (the employment of which is to round out each fragment) with many skips (as in disjunctive music) from one plane of experience to another, resulting in tension and explosion. As such, although it demands the reader's participation in the making of the final scheme, it is, nevertheless, different from the traditional mode in which poetry starts with the total merging of the poet and the objects. Yet, we must also realize that only then can we begin to have a dynamic poetry, a poetry of all-inclusiveness that the existential reality demands of modern Chinese poets, as opposed to the traditional static beauty of single moods and moments.

Wai-lim Yip
1969

Contents

SHANG CH'IN (LO YEN), 1931–.

b.   Szech'uan Province.

Former sergeant; proofreader; Iowa International Writing Program 1969–.

Statement:

The act of writing poetry is by no means different from the act of living. Writing poetry is the best evidence of being a man. Therefore, to demand the explanation of a poem is quite superfluous, because poetry is in itself the explanation of life. The poem is the poet's son, by blood, not adopted; it is the poet's love, the flowering of his pure emotion.

There is no such thing as inspiration. A poem grows out from the various degrees and various phases of saturation of the poet's pure emotion toward life and the cosmos.

Having been a soldier for twenty-odd years, I have never liked war. Fishing is what I like.
I hate to have my hair cut, but I can't ignore it either.
I consider taking a bath the most luxurious comfort.
I am a wine-lover, but my capacity is disappointingly small.
I frequently suffer from insomnia in my pursuit of dreams.
I don't believe in gods, but am inclined to believe in the existence of ghosts.
By gulping down all the scenery and the entire sky, I got stomach trouble.
When I talk, I talk out of the side of my mouth, but even now I am not yet sure which side it is.
Recently, I have begun to fear the fact that I am almost forty.

Shang Ch'in

GRADIENT OF THE MILKY WAY

In the north-north-west of the empyrean
The sheepflock are muteness in file,
One fashion of longing
In another fashion.
The pasture lies in the east of the Milky Way while
The pond in the deep of the heart,
The heart at the corpulent loins of the guitar.

But in one night the Milky Way
With its gradient
Seems to have twisted silence
And lowered its very elemental leaf
To the water
To receive those stars.

The Milky Way lowers itself to the water.
Stars cry out silently.
Many simple limbs and forms
Are moved by their own shadows.
The guitar sails on the sound-wave and
                                the meadow
Drifts under the cordage;
Sheds tears
             and becomes the sister of the pond.

Between the high-tension wire and the grape trellis
The Milky Way stoops toward itself,

That is, straight toward my southeast.
The dead sound of the motor is bound
By two lines of eucalyptus.
                          The mildewed
Sighing becomes a sound-blast at midnight.
My friend asks the way with a cube of sugar
And gets lost in the jungle under the eaves.
No one knows how at sea you were, seeing her wash her hair,

Meanwhile the Milky Way is beneath the pasture;
No one knows how at sea I was, seeing you dry your hair in the sun.
God of the Earth, how boring it is to die!
Time leaks away in the market basket
To become beehives
To make
Honey that tastes sweet only to the blind.

Ever since the Milky Way moved its gradient
To the flat, flat corner of my forehead
In the north-north-west of the empyrean
There is day and night—
     Night gone never returns
     Day come never goes again—
March jolts on our shoulders,
Skirts are burnt by our gaze, pretty bodies
Dissolve in a lane of sunshine,
Leaving the gradient of the Milky Way
In the empty drinking glass.

THE TREE IN A TREE

    How happy are the trees under the eyelashes!
    Seeing, trees in the fog
    At the earlobes touched by the fingers of the fog
    The earlobes being kissed between the teeth by the tongue

    How quiet are the trees at the end of the nose!
    Smelling, trees in the wind
    At the moustache touched by the skirts of the wind
    The moustache being kissed on the lips by the nose-tip

    How brilliant are the trees upon the forehead!
    Weeping, trees in the rain
    On the cheeks touched by the toes of the rain
    The cheeks being kissed at the temples by the long hair

(In the eyes), there are stars in the fog
(In the dew), trembling lightly
(In the ears), there is a rivulet in the rain
(In the winds), weeping lowly

(In the arms) there is fog in the hands
(In the hair) there is wind at the neck
There is rain on the face
Dew on the tip of the nose
Stream in the vale
Road by the stream
Trees in the woods
Heart on the trees
In the tree in the tree
In the tree, there is a tree very sad

Tree in the tree, tree among trees, O that tree in the tree!

THE BLACK CRYSTAL OF NO SUBSTANCE

"We should turn off the light before undressing, otherwise LIGHT will stay on our flesh."

"Because of its hold on you?"

"Because of its being an insulator."

"What about the moon then?"

"Even the stars are the same." After the light is turned off, the curtain falls down; outside the window is nothing but the stiff night. Inside the house a person, after having lost his hair, has lost also his lips and tongue; the arms each from its back and shoulder, from the breasts and waist, disappear; his legs and his ankles go a little bit later. After that, what is left is the so-called BEING.

N'ETRE PAS. They were not being dissolved by darkness; they took part in and purified DARKNESS and thus: Alas, how difficult it is to make a black crystal of no substance.

THE QUEUE BEING UNBRAIDED

Whirled up, the dust is as convulsed as the cordage being stranded
Coiled together, the ropes are as confused as the queue being braided
(This is false)

The queue being unbraided   Early spring dusk   Lying lazy in bed even after 10 a.m.   On the terrace a clog with a broken lace   The queue being unbraided   Under it a slender white neck   A beggar cooling himself at the gate of drainage   A policeman back from night duties   Tinkling of earrings in a hot-spring bath   A disused bomb and a deserted ship

And the hawser on the deserted ship; and the queue being unbraided; and lazy in bed, yawning; and a tear from the right eye flows to the left: "I thought the water in your lake was sweet!" and the tear from the left eye has already passed the ear's door—telling her how slack the evening winds are in the suburbs—and is flowing into the unbraided hair.

THE CAPTAIN

I

You have not seen the icy routes of thought. The colorless dreams are drawn crosswise by you, O captain. *I do not know how he sailed across the three primary colors.* I do not know how you pass from red to yellow, how you pass between two colors. You cannot tell where their boundary is, you cannot tell what latitude and longitude you are now on.

How deep and how blue is the melancholy to starboard!

Before the rainbow that straddles mountains and seas, O captain, I have, too, my own secret worries: if your ship suddenly turns itself into a pier, where, then, can you moor? Or if you, waking up, find the sea become land. . . . Perhaps, I should tell you whence flows my brother's snivel and where the tears of some other's sister pass.

II

The captain, with his back against the sun, sees the eagle of the color of autumn weeds spitting out pointless diamonds and cutting open a pensive young girl's windowpane and splashing into pieces on the silence of February. He remembers the penguins in the poles built up, with the eyesight of the sailors who have ceased sailing for a long time, a whimpering sadness to shroud the port.

GIRAFFE

When the young jailer found that, at the prisoners' monthly physical examination, every time there was an increase in height, it was exclusively in the neck, he reported to the warden, "Sir, the windows are too high." The answer was, "No, it's the years the prisoners are longing for."

The kindly jailer did not know the look of years, did not know the birthplace of years nor the whereabouts of years, and thus, he went night after night to the zoo to wait for them under the giraffe pen.

THE TURNOUT ON A HAIRPIN MOUNTAIN ROAD

At a bend on the silent mountain road, a vacant cab slowed down and stopped unaware of itself the way a leaf, without being blown by the wind, falls off the tree. The young driver suddenly remembered a turnout people called "leaping field." "Yes, leaping field, leaping field." Then he thought of the problems of "higher and lower" and the problems of "hiring and renting"—concerning the soul.

And when he passed the bend a second time, carrying in it some passengers, he suddenly stepped on the brake and, bowing down his head, wept bitterly over the steering wheel, for he thought he had just crashed into the cab which was parked there and into himself still in the driver's seat.

POEM

In the rice-wine-colored evening, upon my incorruptible forehead, inside my eyes, my ears, I cast my shadow before her, covering her completely. She is an engraver. She creates sound inside her own auditory canal. From the very beginning I have said, "I come, not to cast myself into you, but to exit from your hands." But she turned a bust upside down and remolded it, ah, upside down, and so I woke up from daybreak and won over daybreak.

In both her memory and mine, her slender rose hand had already turned a light violet.

FIRE EXTINGUISHER

At a furiously rising noon, I gazed deeply at the fire extinguisher on the wall. A small boy came over and said to me, "Look! There are two fire extinguishers in your eyes." Because of this simple statement, I could not help crying. I saw two *me*'s shedding tears in his eyes. He did not tell me, in the reflection of these tears, how many *him*'s were there.

FOUR LINES ON MUCHA, A SMALL TOWN

Protruberant breasts are like Old Heaven's prominent forehead.
The girl walking in the morning tries you with a light cough, Old Heaven's
Prominent forehead covers the eyes desiring to open. Daybreak.
The eyes desiring to open are blocked by the protruberant breasts.

TAIPEI, 1960

I

Beside the exhausted day and feeling like charcoal I anticipate her breathing her last, using rose crepe paper to kindle the clouds, allowing a half-closed window a fine decoration. Beyond the tile kiln in the distant suburb, a solitary expression of the eyes seems to have burnt and scorched the invisible other side of the mountain.

II

On the main street the day flings its heart out of its bosom and hangs down slowly along the frigid buildings and pacifies us who are looking into the daylight, taking down our sunglasses. The blood in the endocardium is obscurely dark and genial and its amplitude makes him become once again a mole: We are charcoal, not prepared in the tilery, but come to what we are by burning ourselves. If someone walks toward the west, it is only because the wind from the movie screen is also cold and because of this one's desire increases to smoke and drink.

III

Fountainless city, O pitiful sunset, let me praise you by a shower. For a long time I have not spit on others with tears. As to the four obstinate iron beasts, the saliva from their mouths describes for us a hand that can never be retrieved.

IV

In the New Park just above the turnstile a naughty boy, as if to hurry the ants on their way, directs night to come in from this side; meanwhile day goes out from the other.

THE NIGHT BEFORE

"Because the eternal sea has been primeval; ah, you cannot murder a wave, because you cannot murder a moon, because you cannot murder a sun, because you cannot murder your own shadow because . . . ."

At that time I was walking onward stealthily night after night and having heard what I once said I returned hastily from the totally dark, starred sky and saw myself sound asleep by the tear-wet pillow, ho, ho, even the smile was of last year's March.

EMOTION ABOVE SEA LEVEL

After the rainy season has begun, the vultures stop their happy but fear-inspiring whistle in the vacant valley.

How come that you remember a retired ship? Sea oysters making a relief of the anchor, the hilarious shoals unscrupulously returned home empty-handed. A negligent mouse woke up from its two-year's sleep and started to weep on the deck. In truth, you were but a dog in service. A rainy day might not be a day for a holy feast. The good-hearted Prince of India would not give you one of his Hong Kong feet. The wind-hunter came back with nothing but a red bell-shaped nose . . . .

Wait until nightfall when I shall run away for a hundred and eighty minutes, going along the firewood-pickers' path up to the summit where the night, selfish, grudging me even a piece of watermelon, uses my held-back tears to smash into pieces the stars of champagne.

THE MAGUEY

Since you plucked your feet out of the pond
   densely grown with the watercress,
Your wrist watch indicates half-past three,
   pointing to the weed-webbed heart;
And the yew trees are darkly still beneath the floating ash leaves.
  Moon sees weeds
  Ghosts see moon
  Water and moon invisible
  Water and moon immobile

The Goddess Star is a spring on a soldier's rifle, holding
The hazardous Milky Way, my heart's direction.
And eyelashes projected from early spring
Are rainbows above your fictional death.

Thereupon, what remains in my heart is the maguey.
Doctor, why does the oleander bloom incessantly? and
Blooming is sickness, doctor.
This is no desert.
This is the zone for dozing and you are an electric fan;
You are the windshield wipers still working after the car stops.
Only you are the stillness, because you are the only sound.

THE DISTANT LULLABY

Wearily

It may be raining on the island
On your pillow salt is spread to sun
Beyond the window of salt stands the night
Night! The night will be guarding you

Guarding the earth guarding the salt
Guarding you and guarding the trees
Because the earth is guarding the trees
Because the trees will be guarding you

Because the trees will be guarding the night
The birds in the woods guarding the trees
The birds on the trees guarding the stars
The stars in the night are guarding you

Because the stars will be guarding the night
The clouds in the sky guarding the stars
The clouds between the stars guarding the winds
The winds in the night are guarding you

Because the winds will be guarding the night
The grass on the ground guarding the winds
The grass in the winds guarding the dews
The dews in the night are guarding you

Because the dews will be guarding you
Guarding the earth guarding the trees
Guarding the mountains guarding the fog
The fog in the night is guarding you

The fog in the night guarding the river
The water in the river guarding its banks
Guarding the fish guarding the sea
The mountains by the sea are guarding you

The mountains in the night are guarding you
The mountains in the night are guarding the sea
Guarding the beaches guarding the waves
The boat on the waves is guarding you

Guarding the waves guarding the night
Guarding the beaches guarding you
Guarding the river banks guarding the water
In the night I am guarding you

Guarding the mountains guarding the night
Guarding the earth guarding you
Guarding the stars guarding the fog
In the night I am guarding you

Guarding the woods guarding you
Guarding the grass guarding the night
Guarding the winds guarding the fog
In the night I am guarding you

Guarding the voices guarding the night
Guarding the birds guarding you
Guarding the wars guarding death
In the night I am guarding you

Guarding forms and guarding you
Guarding speed and guarding night

Guarding shadows guarding the dark
In the night I am guarding you

Guarding solitude and guarding night
Guarding distance and guarding you
In the night I am guarding the night
In the night I am guarding you

THE ESCAPING SKY

The deadman's face is a swamp unseen by men;
A swamp in the wasteland is the escape of part of the sky.
The fugitive sky is the brimming of roses;
The brimming of roses is the snow that has never fallen.
The fallen snow is a string being twanged;
A string being twanged is a tear in the veins.
The rising tears are burning hearts;
And burning hearts are swamps, their wastelands.

DOOR OR SKY

Time   being disputed.

Place   not a bit of sky.
       bankless moat encloses
       roofless enclosure.

Cast   an unwatched prisoner.
       (close by the enclosure a road walked into by this prisoner.)
       on the road walking, this prisoner.
       finally, he leaves the road built by his footsteps.

He foots toward center of enclosure;
With hands cuts down several trees within it.

With teeth and hands
With trees and vines cut down by hands and teeth
He makes a door
A door which is a mere frame.
(And ties it onto a large tree.)

He examines it for a long while.
He thinks about it for a deep moment.

He pushes door;
He goes out . . .

He goes out, a few steps, returns
He pushes door again.
He goes out.
Out—come.
Out—go.

Not a bit of sky, and under it, bankless moat that encloses barb wires that enclose roofless enclosure that encloses within, under two feet, a road—walked into by an unwatched prisoner—that encloses a distant center. This unwatched prisoner pushes open a door made by his own hands, a mere frame

Out—go
Out—come
Out—go
Out—come. Out—go. Out—go. Out—come. Out—come. Out—go.
Out. out. out. out. out. out.

Until we see the sky.

CHENG CH'OU-YÜ (CHENG WEN-T'AO), 1933–.

b.   Honan Province.

Employed in the Port Bureau in Taiwan; Iowa International Writing Program, 1968–69; teaching assistant, Department of Chinese, The University of Iowa, 1969–.

Poetry: *Upon the Dreamland* (1955)
       To Pass On the Mantle (1966)
       Slave Girls Outside the Windows (1968)

Statement:

Poetry does not represent depression directly. Depression stops at deep thinking and, after it has been recognized, rises into a special gesture, natural but uncommon.

The poet in the making of a poem, must, at the same time, grasp and develop the special quality of the voice inherent in his own race. In fact, every word (character) is a sign of meaning in this sense.

Poetry of absolute beauty is never rough, except when the poet deliberately makes an absolute beauty of roughness.

THE MAN ON THE MOTORCYCLE

Every evening he rides by this street of houses
The women leaning in doorways in time of war
Like seeing this hurry-scurry
And a cap cocked in the rising dust

Where does this man come from
Who does not go off to war?
The motorcycle goes by in the evening in time of war
The women leaning in doorways
Ruminating

A MORNING SCENE

The newly-widowed November comes,
Veiled in gray nylons. O Season of Rains!
Are you in doubt? The occasional November sun is free of cosmetics.

No curve is developed from the harbor's blueprint but translucence.
A milky mailboat from Europe,
Like the university dormitory in autumn,
The coeds wearing the variegated wools,
Red, yellow, and green pennants, going to—
Ai, ai, they must be the coeds who have just enrolled as freshmen
The ones apt to smile, blush, and look curiously here and there.

SLAVE GIRLS OUTSIDE THE WINDOWS

The Square Window

A little square of night sky, a sapphire blue and an oriental lustre make me a Persian. If it were basted on my headdress, wiped and wiped by slave girls, I would begin thinking of burying it and to bury it I have to do nothing but to close my eyelashes. It becomes the somberly blue passage of the tomb-palace. I decide to hold the slave girls by their hands and, kissing them one at every step, I come out.

The Round Window

The small ring of sunlit sky is glazed. Like a plate, it always holds just such a cloud. To dine alone is something craved by the young. *Ai!* what I am expecting is the arrival of the night, since when the night comes, empty glasses will have wine and, appearing from the plates will be those slave girls . . . the ones, for not having moved about frequently, are always elephantine.

The 卐 Window[1]

I am a god facing the south, my naked east-arm bound with the night of gauze and, hanging on my wrist, the stars, my slave girls.

A god's slave girls never go unnamed, but as I take one I may forget one, and call them a wrong name sometimes, or embrace them in my four limbs to let them turn, like a windmill, and vying for wind with their over-whelming whispers.

THE PROPHET OF NAKEDNESS

To be naked together with a mailboat in the tropical bay
The good-looking muscle of this steel animal
Was striped with some green tattoo
I remember I did not put on anything
(Not even a stripe of tattoo)
If not for the shadow of some Chinese red trees
I would be stunned to death by the long-feathered sea birds

---

[1] A mystic Buddhist emblem for good fortune and virtue, and, because of this, many windows and balustrades are worked into this pattern in China. There is nothing Nazi about this swastika emblem here.

At that time I was a sailor thrown here and there
Because I have sniffed off the shadows of all travelers to brew wine
I disdain those sojourners pretending to cover their lower limbs
To leave behind too many children
O when spring comes, this naked body of mine, drinking wine, will be
      beautiful like a red coral

WHEN GAILY DRESSED UP

If I were you, I would patrol the lane in a dark night
And stop at the door, where there is weeping, to find Death,
Approach it and plant my lapel-flower
On the head, stark and cold but a moment ago.
I come out of the dancing party, puzzling:
For whom the great hall is emptied? I wait on the doorsteps,
Where there is weeping, so that the soul just coming out of its cell
May be bribed with my fragrance into telling me:
For whom is death left, for whom the great hall is emptied?

I wish I could find, when gaily dressed up,
At the place where there is weeping,
The soul not yet decomposed.
How I wish (even if to die is to go to hell)
I could know this point for sure
So that I will go to tomorrow's party, to bear with girls and the
      emptied great hall.
Ai, if I were you, a beautiful boy besotted with pleasure.

MISTRESS

In a little town of green stone lives my mistress
I leave her nothing
But a furrow of gold chrysanthemums and a high, high window

Which perhaps will let in some desolation
Perhaps . . . and chrysanthemum is patient.
Desolation and patience, I think, are good for women
So every time I go there I wear a suit of blue clothes
I want her to feel this is the season or
A migrant bird coming
Because I am one of those who seldom comes home

THE MOUNT OF MIGHT: IMPRESSIONS

Unable to go farther east, fearing our toes might kick into the soft
    belly of the early sun
We walk into a line of fish under the corridor of the sky,
Unable to go farther west, west being the ridgepole of happiness.

Meteorites strike on our shoulders of coarse linen.
Water gurgles from the native town of stars.
And mountains, bud-like, lock the flowers
Under our bare feet,
Unable to go farther ahead, ahead being sky's end.

Great pines larkspurred
Are pooled by white clouds.
Although we can live forever by casting the fishing line,
We cannot forget the tattered road we came by.
       Void and void and void
       We do not hope to turn our heads
       And once we ferry ourselves over there
       We'll be where we turn our heads

BOAT OF TEN OARS

Peinan Mountains: the hunting season already floats on rains.
Like a sudden rapport with the River of Lu at night:

Savagery crossing troops about to touch,
Body-coolness of a witch who has muffled all her craft.

Be light . . . and lighter, to row our ten oars.
I am afraid that night is already disturbed,
Which, breezily, sticks to our front breasts like a whirlpool of hair.

PEI-A-NAN, AN ABORIGINAL VILLAGE

My wife is a tree, so am I;
And my wife is an excellent spinning wheel
Whose shuttles of squirrels spin the drifting clouds.
Up on high: what she loves to spin is those clouds.

And how I wish my job to be
Ringing my bosom's
        grade-school bell,
Because I have reached this age—
When woodpeckers stand on my shoulders.

AUTUMN SACRIFICE

Night stills down: valleys close up.
No more women's drumming of shuttles because hunters have returned.
After the moon has risen, hunters get drunk
And become priests looking up
To the eaves of the sanctuary
Autumn-tainted, scattering like dewdrops.

Beneath the eaves, wooden altars tremble.
Naked sheep are covered slovenly with grass.
Like delicate throbbing,
Wandering spirits of drunk pheasants and bats
Doltishly come out from the kitchen range.

NU-NU-CHIA-LI-T'AI, MOUNTAIN OF DRIFTING CLOUDS

Winds whirl up hair like black will-o'-the-wisp.
I am being heaped too high:
Above the burning head, a sallow mountain moon.

Curly home-thoughts burnt into green smoke,
Wind-drenched, so strong and fragrant
That stars smelling it would reel and reel to fall.

Wind stops. Moon vanishes. Flames dissolve into flying frost
And flying frost moistens plants
And plants are like myself. Thinking thus, my corpse.

GRASS TO WEAVE AUTUMN

I

Trying to weave autumn's mornings and nights
As with blades of straw
Weaving left and right, sandals to hurry along.

Look! Wildgeese, wearing mornings and nights, have hurried here.
I come to think: much of geese's memory
Is the wintered and summered hustle and bustle.

II

Autumn morning on the island is always hung with
Patches and patches of chrysanthemum's yellow, palm's brown.

And on my transparent board is the North drawn by you
Where earth's coarseness is pressed flat
And wind-sand and ideals turn fine,

When I remember, like herds of running horses,
Wheat ripens, ripening in September
Under the herdsman's whip of wind.

Oh, North
Ancient grindstones
Year after year grinding new wheat.

III

That I did not embroider anything you knew.
And yet the rope stranded from my heart's silk
Is always trailing with parting days.

Is it mist that gathers into dews or dews sprayed into mist?
And who lets us have nothing but quarrels between sun and moon?

A bundle of parting days
Like yellow flowers set in the year's empty vase.
Should the setter be you, O Autumn:
I would happily receive them.

IV

Moon finishes rounding itself: late autumn already.
I want to say: this year's west wind comes too early.

For days on end, capitals let themselves loose on festivals.
Suddenly I have a desire to return:
Why should the Double-Tenth [1] Day come before the Double-Ninth?–

[1] The Double-Tenth Day falls on October 10, a date to commemorate the founding of the Republic which is observed every year with great festivity. The Double-Ninth Day falls on the ninth day of the ninth month, i.e., on the lunar calendar which the Chinese had used until the solar system, a Western invention, was adopted, along with Mr. Democracy and Mr. Science, by the Republic. All Chinese festivals, like the Double-Ninth Day, are still being scrupulously observed by the people in spite of

Thinking of the port of October, where
In the sky's blue, much strolling clouds,
On the sea, much white waves.

I want to ascend some height to view you—the sealand has been solitary.
Striving to bloom and break
Bursting into white flowers all over, and yielding no fruit.

BORDER TAVERN

Autumn's frontier, divided under the same sunset.
Where lands meet, yellow chrysanthemums silently stand.
And he came from faraway, drinking in sobriety.
Ouside the window, foreign land.

O to stride outside, one mere step is nostalgia,
That beautiful nostalgia, within a hand's reach.

Or, be drunk
(He is an enthusiastic taxpayer.)

Or, spit out singing
Not just standing there like new chrysanthemums
Standing there against the border.

---

the adoption. And the Double-Ninth Day often comes after the Double-Tenth Day which is observed according to the solar calendar!

About the Double-Ninth Day: Huan Ching was told by his teacher that a deadly disaster would befall him on the ninth day of the ninth month. To avoid this, he was to have his family members make embroidered bags to hold dogwoods which were to be fastened onto their shoulders. They were to ascend a high mountain where they would have to drink chrysanthemum wine. Huan did as he was told. He returned home in the evening and found all his domestic fowls dead. Poets like to observe this day by going up the highest peak to drink wine and compose poetry. This is also a day for observing rites for the dead.

GRASS-BORN LAND

spring   spring   *allegro agitato*   still song's time-bird*
the beauty walks on the grass
         white nightjar jumps over toes
         red nightjar jumps over toes   that beauty
thus lies naked in the beast's breast
         thus freely, white hand over breast hair
         wind-like breast hair   wind, like musical variations
blows through the pipe fingers

alas!   already sick
the third month   long as the food-finding elephant trunk
like a stethoscope sounding the breast   and sunset like a flower-drum
the kind of waist   upon which half-hangs the flower-drum
         which should be covered by a grass skirt
grass-skirt-like waterfall   waterfall-like buildings
        transparent   moving   opens and closes (windows for fish-viewing)
alas!   she is sick   what has the third month planted inside her waist?
(is it that the third month is urging marriage?)
if so . . . marry the east wind   because of the peach-blossom kind of
sickness   hiding red into bud   disclosed by the first breeze of east wind

this year   herbs and grasses all frozen
green maidens (whichever complexion)
laughed at by pine needles in dark corners
so the beauty with a white lily planted between lips
hawking along rooftops like clouds
(with a bundle of lilies one can go around the world)
this year   the largest customers
are still those from chimneys—husbands like flighty smoke
       tickling smoke   tickling like young sisters
            tinkling laughs by the moneybag
            so to make the mistaking lilies thought

*The time-bird is a legendary bird that tells the different watches of the night.

husbands bought after some striving abound in coins   but in fact
                       in husbands' pockets there tinkles
                       the keys to chastity belts

alas!   she is so sick   like a dancer
lies upon the grass-born land   that beauty
with four trees experiments evolution
and those bee-sisters who learnt from her all their life
also moves back and forth between red flowers and white flowers
selects, refines the genius of sex
            creates the genius of pillows   creates pillows of dreams
            dreams like cooking art   homemade   with fear
              minding to suit the taste of whoever . . .

spring   spring   *allegro agitato*   spring   still song's time-bird
the first watch   east wind that has chewed the deer's horns   already dead
in the thin groom's orgastic swell   the second watch   the redeemed beauty
walks out of her waterfall   she is a kind of fruit
body fragrance inside a cell   ashamed of being an organ of the grass skirt
         (when two naked bodies meet, don't they become clothes to each?)
allegro agitato   spring   spring   beginning of the third watch
that beauty   leaning flat upon unsewable sickness
        one kind of language sewed the two lips
          a language she likes to hear likes to speak first
          a language   a dose wrongly given
will be her wedding dress (besides her sickness
        who can do what for her wedding's nakedness?)
and then   at the end of the third watch   almost the fourth
night upon the grass-born land   loosely covering
she walks at will   at will picks a lily and sits down
        when the lily is planted between her lips
        she, like a mother just given birth to a child
        happily boasts of the pains remembered
spring   spring singing toward the fifth watch makes night already old
flowing over her fish-white wrinkles   gray-haired dawn flows like tears
              so rolling   so helpless after the rolling
              so happy to die of sickness

spring   spring singing all over the third month remains to be herself
like the beauty's toes   white nightjar jumps over   red nightjar jumps over
wind goes   music of pipes gone   this is the body she would do no self-injury
this is needle   piercing through every leaf
this is the man   a mid-man is what she means

LO FU (MO LO-FU), 1927–.

b.   Hunan Province.

Liaison officer in the Chinese Navy; coffee-shop owner; editor of the *Epoch Poetry Quarterly* (with Chang Mo and Ya Hsien).

Poetry: *The Spiritual River* (1958)
        Death in the Stone Cell (1964)
        Poems of Beyond (1967)

Statement:

What we see in the mirror is not the image of modern men, but their merciless destinies against which writing poetry is a form of revenge. That is why the language of my poetry often enrages the gods and makes people aware of the stark fact that to live is to stand in the flow of blood. Unfortunately, I am a humanist, too anxious to deliver men from the prison of their consciousness. From my poetry they can get the greatest freedom.

I suddenly find that I am so meager that there is practically nothing in my life that is worth mentioning except writing poetry.

MY BEAST

Crouched always in my coverless body
My beast
With his brown tongue blocks my lips about to scream
Those flashing pupils, perhaps my presentiments
To murder my wedding night
God, on veins of a judas tree
You would smell corpses in Picasso's gallery
God, in the ancient tower of Muzot
You would touch the iciness of Rilke's eyes

My beast is a nice bridegroom
You would read much from his hairs
He always clasps your voice, puts on your clothes
And comes and goes in the dust
His hoofs! God, are resonant with your angry words

Those are the mornings—
My beast inlays my girdle with its teeth
Pushes me toward the terrace
To see where wick flowers on the island had dropped
To see how last night's moon was strangled by seaweeds
And to demand tides of
The long-necked Grecian bottle treasuring weeping
God, why does he want me to speak out
Whether the owner of the wrecked ship still proudly cultivates some beard
Who lurks behind the reefs
To tempt me to sing: *That Brown Little Jug*

God, you must have seen
How he abused your words
My beast
Without feeling a bit sorry about it
Embroiders your name on a blanket of a landlady next door
Allows some casual women to lie on it
Teasing, deliberately, your humility
And hangs it on a clothesline like a pair of torn socks

Sunday. Many narrow doors are open
My beast
Forces me to climb into the church through a window
Instigates me to pluck out blood-nails from Jesus' palms
And allows candles to light up the lowness on my face
When all the penitent men have left
He hides the tear vases brimful of pity and skulks away ahead of me
God, he positively said
He was your handsome neighbor

In the season of narcissus
My beast, free-winging and refined
Teaches me how Li Po floated his satin boots in the wine jug
      how Byron gambled away one leg, writing poetry
He says: pale smiles
Should be nailed to death on pale cheeks
Dark long tunes should crush into pieces at Schubert's bed
God,
He even wants me to count stars through a layer of cloth
And, counting, to swear at so-and-so a drab
But on the thoroughfare in Burma
He reads to the public the scripture carved on a rock
My beast, my nice bridegroom . . .
His laughs are soft, wind-soft

If on a certain island
On a certain island I should die
My beast
Would not prepare any clothes for my corpse
He would cover me with his huge palm
He would not even leave on my neck such a fissure
As to allow a small piece of butterfly wing to fall through
I walk into your black curtain, naked thus
God,
Before your altar of judgment, I don't even have a thread to cover
      my shame

completed a building.
as of spring
ipped of their skeletons,
vling on the ground—
stealing the sun.

parapets.
gun case.
rrow's countenance.
d in hanging,
ne is too crude.

ody in the dugouts,
lasma exchanging reputations

ne sun doesn't come out from the

rals.

t and obstinacy in its

sort of animal,
hat forever defies folding.
e my roof,
es eaten once by the cuttlefish.

f serpents,
bedsheet;
yebrows tomorrow's worries,
n eyes for the first time—
ain unknown men.

When on the rooftrees shreds of the soul are walking
Aurora attracted: you said I did not belong to perfection
Aurora attracted: God, your windows are moving
My reason climbs, rising in your splendor
And on the prisoners' numbered clothes
       is carved the gray stillness I no longer remember
And my beast breeds maggots in human virginity
Your love has since decayed and smelt

God,
Let your toes reach out from the rock
I have read all your trees
And known in whose conception they grow
I have tasted every blade of grass
One blade of grass is one vein in your blood

And my beast
He knows only himself, licking all his scales
Unlike me
Always prostrate so as to kiss the passing shadow of your robe
God,
He wants to trample secretly on your harvest
And live permanently inside my body
And nestle in my eyes

Like Judas at the supper biting greedily
Lord's last smile on the plate
God,
My beast, the same way he wants to gnaw at me
(Have you ever seen locusts cry?
And so completely nothing is left in me)
Because he said positively
He is your handsome neighbor, my bridegroom

DEATH IN THE STONE CELL *
(Selections)

1

Merely lifting my head toward a neighboring lane, I am stupef
In the morning, a man rebels against death with his naked body
And allows a black tributary to roar in his veins
I am stupefied: my eyesight sweeps past a stone wall
And chisels on it two troughs of blood.

My face spreads like a tree; the tree grows in the fire.
All quiet but pupils move behind the eyes,
Toward directions people dare not talk about:
I am indeed a sawed-off bitter pear tree
On whose annual rings you can still hear clearly winds and cicadas

2

To all knocking at the door the door-rings answer with glorious bus
of the past
As all my brothers will come and drink my foreheadful of anxiety:
Your thirst is like a white flower in my room;
I have to open my eyes only slightly and there will be sound
Tinkling from the walls down on the plates served to guests.
And afterwards an afternoon of bitter arguing and all kinds of unclea
revelations—
Your language is a heap of unwashed clothes,
Being hurt always like people without a constant home.
When the tree's profile is split by the light of a stone crevice,
Its height gives me the stature of a building's firmness.

5

Matches, a blast of flame, embrace the entire world.
Before city is burnt, a desperado is born in hurrahs.

*When these translations were made, the book of the same title in which the poet mad
some changes was not published. I followed essentially their earlier versions, excep
for Number 1, of which the revised version is definitely better.

18

Don't spit in my face, brothers, for having
You will wake up from winter like pajam
And will be like fallen teeth and woods st
So weak, so much like the grass roots cra
The blood-lost rock will be flagellated for

Always teased, I am a citadel, a pit on the
Romanticism paints my soul on a red-hot
Today's voice will be congealed into tomo
If on the verandah only an incomplete hea
All of you will hurrah because the guilloti

19

And so you divide the feast of your own b
Like doctors who write their theses with p
for eyeballs,
When guests leave the session one by one,
There will be no more discussion why t
gun barrel
So as to let war write biographies for gene

Finding complaisance in a lizard's eyesigh
skin complexion,
At noon, I thought you could be the same
And thought of war—war is a black skirt
When death kicks in two the rainbow abo
I suddenly remember you had a pair of ey

22

Gloria, Pucelage, etc., being aftergrowths
We are always wrapped up in a notorious
When a mother puts in between a baby's e
The bride, too—the hazard in some drunke
Will be bitten on her wedding night by cer

On happy festivals we say our thanks by scoffing
And take the sun as the only harvest of summer.
O God, how can we swallow your forebodings,
How can we make a supper from giving away,
And let them express their full pride with their tongues?

If we happen to meet each other on the "tomb-sweeping" day, sisters,
Can you refrain from playing my spirit like a colorful canopy?
We give reins once more to our failure upon the unsmiling face.
While part of the flying paper ash is forgetting,
Another part of it is found in some sober new land.

You always try to reason men's satisfaction by your eyes,
Flattery being lichens on the stone well—
                      a slip of my feet,
My desire would be smashed into a heap of dead animals.

35

Sound and countenance coming toward me from the front, I look up
With the absorption of one taking a shower, receiving its regard
With my parched lips.
In order to tell where to put this ladder
I jump up a second time to glance at the sun rise the sun set.

How sour! this color, always tempting us to grope in a certain direction,
And following its turns, to pursue it along the veins of a leaf.
If all flowers were faithful to spring but disgraced themselves to autumn,
We would wait ruefully in order to hear the one real cry
From the fruit shell when it cracks.

36

Up from the somber side of a tract of the face the sail rises,
Remembering sand hills and the footprint among footprints.
The sail rises, telling a kind of surplus suffering,
Blue, Blue, Blue, Blue, Blue, Blue,
Eventually there will be a sea drowned in the hands of this woman.

Lo Fu

Toes striking lightly, you keep a star's location by swimming backstroke.
But turning over abruptly you are lost in a sadness, neither blue nor black.
Let me follow you, for your sceptre, for the nuance of your laugh
For your very first one, that has been poisoned to death by that girl
With her complaisance in her raised eyebrows.

40

At the end of the corridor, you are that tomb
Once again in your eyes, earlier than I—
Take off tendons and bones, put on dust.
You want to resist, with another fashion of sleep,
The tempest arising from a woman loosening her hair.

He hides in his flesh such a metaphor:
My bones are soft, being fed by gastropod's juice.
War, swings among us like a black sock.
Thinking of 'dead' and 'not dead,'
My eyesight becomes very beastly, very *Hemingway*.

41

And morning is a beetle that walks on its back,
Chewing as it goes on. I am the leftover night,
Barely hearing stars crying among the joints of teeth.
I write my dying commands on the wind and on the sun about to rise,
And only by sneezing can I remember what eats me is myself.
On the forehead there is propped up a black tent, like a tear lodging
           on the cheek.
I walk into the sun and come out of the sunflower,
Not knowing whether wearing green clothes would look like clouds,
Which being single, grow lean from sickness in a valley.
After I finish carving death on the tombstone, I break the knife in two.

42

Sisters can fumble out some love even from palm reading.
The red-faced god, who supports the ground structures with soft cheek-bones,

Sends out all sorts of fun through the tip of the tongue. And you are
        crinkled flowers
Thrown away by those gone and taken up again by those coming—
You are sounds of shoes that die on the streets and wake on the streets.

Like a great serpent sloughing off its skin
The city of spring scatters blood-stained scales.
You come around to see, then complain: the streets' surface is not
        bright enough,
Tempting me to scoop out one of my eyes to supplement it.
O God! What I can offer before your feet is but this much anger.

HEARSAY OF APRIL (NO. 3)

Build all the tombs in the ear, to hear clearly
Your bootfalls after going off to the frontier.
All roses wither in one night, just as your names
Become a pile of numbers in war, just as your weariness
Can no longer remember which city once crumbled in my heart.

Why silent prayer? We no longer have eyes to close,
No longer find our seventh day in the burning.
Winter: we ought to live forever in ourselves.
Snow: we ought to enter into our ears, take off our clothes
To cover our naked sons.

THE FIRST-BORN BLACKNESS

Unable to tell yet whose hand it is—your door opening slowly,
I flash into your pupils and drink the blackness in them.
You are the root and fruit, holding a thousand years in one core.
We make a circle and dance and get fire from it,
And thus I am burnt by the blackness of your pupils.

You pave a road from your eyebrows leading to morning
Morning, receiving the fall of another star, wakes up.
To prove pain is the echo of your coming or the footprint of your going,
You close your eyes to carve your own silence
So quiet that we cannot open our eyes.

To be naked: is this the reason you have for your arrival?
Daughter, before I knew you I had tasted the salt in your eyes
Inside your mother's womb you had learned how to wake up
And how with your fingers to knead time into sound on your little bed
And thrust with your palms to push day back into night.

We have been clothed with light, with the clearness of a lotus.
We have been dazzled by death and the moving stillness of a nave.
And you are the road of yesterday, one rut among the thousands,
When the dinner tray is holding your future,
You are greedily eating our present.

Structured from some gestures of sleep and a whole black night,
You are an oyster, whose two shells draw in the roaring sea.
O Crying! I live to swallow what gives voice.
Let me, steadily, walk out of your pupils
And announce to all the hair: *I am this blackness.*

The world is an armless sleeve: your arrival is wanting in everything.
You stretch two palms, stretching to grasp a tomorrow.
You are the first-born blackness; one flash is a swank banquet.
All the guests look at you with prickly eyes—
To grow a Bo tree in your pupils.

BEYOND THE WHIP

Swing of whip.
Drumming of hoofs becomes color of mountain never to turn back.

Ride together with a thousand mountains.
My horse eats scenery as it goes
And kicks three roadside dogwoods
Into five.

Gallop! Speed roars under hoofs.
I look up at myself at sky's end.

Five or three flowers? Forget it.
I am the bell already rung, truly tired of turning my head to ask
Who—the fallen dust inside those eyes.
      Fallen dust is thoughts of home.

BEYOND SMOKE

Call your name in the surge; your name is
Already beyond a thousand sails.

Tides come, tides go.
Left shoe's print only afternoon.
Right shoe's print already evening.
The month June is at heart a very sentimental book.
The ending is so sadly beautiful
—Setting sun sinks westward.

You still gaze
At a patch of pure white in his eyes.
He kneels toward you toward yesterday toward a cloud-bud beautiful
                the whole afternoon.
Sea, why lit up among other lamps
Just this one of fumes of frenzy?

What else can we grasp?
That which has been called snow, your eyes,
Is now called
Smoke.

YEH SHAN (WANG CHING-HSIEN), 1940–.

b.   Taiwan Province.

Ph.D. candidate in comparative literature at the University of California, Berkeley.

Poetry: *Water's Brim* (1960)
       Flower Season (1963)
       Lantern Boat (1966)
       Selected Poems (1969)

Statement:

A poet should learn to refrain from making statements about poetry. He writes poetry.

————from a letter to Yip Wai-lim

NEWS

None. At the port, I use a pair of compasses
To measure my paleness.

On the way home, many bird corpses,
Many round eyes, bulging and smiling;
Some gunmen are wiping sweat in the teahouse,
Looking at the scenery . . . .

It's the ninth time we used clouds as a topic in our conversation.
Nonetheless, this fool is always beautiful—
The moss on flagstones is killed by continuous sitting.
All chimneys are counted.
She still loves to smile, still very pretty.

One hundred and seven times, clouds used as topics!
She still loves to smile, still pretty.
On the road still many bird corpses.
Some gunmen are still wiping sweat, in the teahouse,
Looking at the scenery . . . .

BUTTERFLY-BOW

I

O drizzling South!
Your eyes glitter, making a feast of me
With the postures of seven snakes
Standing for an instant
Before the greenless wind
From carved curves
Toward sky beyond sky

When midnight retreats, rumbling, leaving me sleepless
On the disorderly wakeful bed

O drizzling South!
You are the prodigous Carmen beyond the door
When you go away, leaving me two lips
When the calm after storm steeps and engulfs me

Your familiar name is falling off
The long-winded good-bye, changed and changed,
Finally returns to stillness
Finally you become the bent hand
Upholding abruptly my momentary anxiety

II

Cover me hard with all autumn's red leaves
Dusking year's winds usher you toward the north
You emerge with the shadow of your back
When stars rise stars sink
Seven colors encircle me
Your tactile sense, all abrupt, shudders toward me
All my thoughts, like a comb, move south to your eyebrows' tips
Here: some black gauze for you, old friend, for memorial

A soldier sitting down against a roaring palm tree
Is making a boat of dried leaves
All the children from the church throw at you
Roses of melancholy
Your dark eyes contract me, contract me

III

Two eyes move here a thousand mountains a million waters
Among them, the soul, O reinless wanderer!
With two wings, with 'modern' sadness you puzzle me
When love belongs to nothing but the convulsed lips of May
You are the eternity rolled up (eternity inside children's eyes)
Remember the twists and turns of evening, your shadow—
Your shadow upon the red tree trunk

I pare away spring
In the shadow think of good-bye jingling in the fiery sun
Helplessness thrown about the sand. You said—
Every night I look up to your name, you chin in the smoke-mist

The corn grows as parasite beneath tombstones, O drizzling South!
Because the bone ash grows
Darkly covering up your footprints
Sorrow pierces everything
With its noiseless rocking, broadcasts
Their nightlong cry

You, asleep, are the sea
Seaweeds and aquatic creatures, your easy and distant poses

FEET

Come with me into cicada's buzz, into anxiety.
Lift our heads to count the horses on votive tablets
Kicking up dust of buckthorn color.
At the water brim count his age, Sound Sleeper!
Your hands are great serpents.

He walks past palaces like the sun's moving shadow,
Ever rising,
Rising to where I sit leg-crossed,
The empty space left for me,
Yesterday's me.

Where we drank water before, you now stand.
I turn my head to look at you:
Green water flows away.
Travelers' lips flow away.
Give me ash, give me loneliness in the midst of clamor.
Forthcoming stars and moons are rosary beads.
You, bidding them, put out the lamp that leads to me.

North-north-west. Beautiful person on the lookout.
Coming out of the forest, do you hear stars howling in the east?
The moon slants toward the right; we speed across the river.

FOR ALICE

At noon, you paused at a bowshot;
Rocked me with your eyes' waves.
Blown over were your outcry, my sigh.
Anger hid behind two pupils
And dripped down with autumn rains.

The last lamp was yours. I fell down abruptly,
Buried among the uneven cards in a game of bridge.
Sitting by the sea wall,
I counted a whole city of lights.

Your cheeks were indescribable.
The second year, they burnt your lung lobes, your window curtains,
Together with a bell's ding dong
Slated on his bleeding wound.
O Alice, when you kneel down with closed palms.
Seven stars move by themselves across my little skylight.

On the parapets are hung some lanterns.
Do you feel the gradually weakening sound?
In the drumming of hooves.
In the bowing over-clasped hands.
Take off your wigs, lovely Alice,
Let me see you of brown color,
You of Lisbon.

CAMPING OUT

Rattling of drums to the right.
Birds in the thick, all-embracing
Desperation, desperation, desperation.

Yesterday's thudding of guns has not yet returned.
When should we wade across the river?
To the deserted castle to smoke
And doze; think of yesterday's eyes,
Someone's eyes.

Pillowing butterflies.
South's lowest star dangles by our ear's edge
The moment we turn to poke the fire.
O you guy, mountains are swelling from your forehead.

NARCISSUS

Stars gone cry out silently behind us.
We argue bitterly over nothing;
Lie down; and in the lullaby
I count stars as they fall into the bottom of the valley,
              turn into fireflies,
Float by our ankles of flower-shadows.

Alas, perhaps deserted mountains and wild ford—
And we share one boat:

Glide down Time's long river;
Flash across seven oceans.
A thousand years: one dream. Immense waves.
Turning my head: you have two temples of star flowers.
Narcissus looks down at himself from Greek Classics.
—Today's stars cry out silently behind us.
We sit down facing each other beneath the north window.
In the dark we pass around yellowing letters to read.

STRAWBERRY FIELDS IN SUMMER

Diggers rest beneath trees.
Tree shadows slowly slants eastward.
Searchers of butterfly-orchids are clambering
A snow-white precipice. Forests in the distance
Look as if growing in a previous century.
Small birds clamor, like a waterfall
A waterfall without any sense of seasons.

I sit inside a small cabin, watching
Several acres of strawberries.
You know, these are several acres of sweetness!
Summer love congeals into
A full valley of juicy red.

And the sun becomes whiter and whiter.
Cicadas' buzz gets more and more on our nerves:
Echoes all four directions; in them
Some degree of primitive sadness.
But mountains and valleys of juicy red
Are no longer the strawberries of former times.

INTO THE MOUNTAINS

Is there yet memory of the deep sea? Corals, aquatics?
If all the sea blue can be planted in a pot,
Our village will be even more gorgeous:
Along the window, twelve pots of full summer.
Fruits ripen rapidly, fowls sing,
Or sensations—merely strings and strings of
Bubbles inevitably rising to the surface.

O Bubbles! Indolent and tired garden-keeper!
O Garden-keeper! counts and counts, records and records,
Never quite remembered how much harvest
We ought to have this year.

When the red-faced man comes—
He comes on his bike—all the florists in the market place will
                put on lined jackets,
All absorbed in drawing their spontaneity
—The seven villages surrounding the capital
Produce practically nothing, but every year
Huge, huge, yellow chrysanthemums bloom and bloom.

Arrange pots of full summer; wave the fan:
Thus, in a brown study, stroll on.
A song is rising bubbles; so are rings of smoke
The garden-keeper puffs. Is there yet memory of the deep sea?
And corals and aquatics?

Our thanksgiving offering to gods, our drums—
These may have no meaning
No meaning, when you climb up by yourself
A permanent, snow-capped mountain. Flashing knives of aborigines.
Baskets some girls discarded after drawing water.
Plank paths along precipices.

I am a blade of seaweed
(Of the deep sea is there . . . .)
O I am ocean currents
A tattooed brave man, O brave man
Once in the mountains, my waist girded with a red scarf,
I will not be one of the clansmen to guard the autumn harvest.
Breaking of waves washes away all the summer feeling
While clamor of mountain winds
Drifts into a tract of sea-coolness.

WASTELAND OF YELLOW CABBAGE FLOWERS

After a shower of rain, how the little blue flowers should
Actively open toward the church window.
Flying birds, tired, fall down. Curves of eaves.

Yeh Shan

If the corridor so damp, damp till our National Double-Five Day,[1]
We would not wait to
Walk the melon fields

Emotions strive to bloom like cabbage flowers.
Blooming, no solemn purpose, but
To express a kind of mature reluctance.
If there were long long roots, reach down to fathom
Some news from the Yellow Spring,
The mineralogy from the center of earth, and Ceres

"I strolled toward the waterfront. Yesterday. Yes,
Until I reached my friend's seaside castle,
Read pictorials, lunched
And listened to news and weather reports from the U.S. Army Radio Station.
A girl broadcasts from Tainan and introduces
A series of hit songs . . ."

I did not go back, talking aimlessly about return, and
Walk near the wasteland of yellow cabbage flowers.
No memory, no memory of two arms of tenderness.
Water snakes and summer clothes of reeds
"Yes, toward the waterfront" he said "let's stroll"
Or to grow some trees, to see on the rolling barley fields
Green strangeness
Beautiful startle!

VARIATION

Wait for warm winds to cool
Like waiting for torrential rain at year's end
Like peeking at bird-singing beyond windbreaks by the reservoir.
This is us, boring stars.

[1] The Double-Five Day is the fifth day of the fifth moon on the lunar calendar. It is a festival in memory of the death of Chü Yuan (343–285 B.C.), China's first great poet. In southern China, the Double-Five Day, or Dragon-Boat Festival, usually falls in a very wet season.

In a different kind of time
Stillness, compared to pursuit,
Is wearier. This is us.
Foolish sunflowers' ambiguous gaze
Golden silence
And abundance like autumn harvest
Bundled along the river.

As to those initiated by chance,
Or cries of hawks and orioles
All related to bows and arrows,
This is you, floating
In the midst of evening mist
Above green mountains.

THE FEEL OF RAIN

Dampness on neck
Spreads; rises from waist.
Hair is jungle's
Climate—
Moss-grown wilds
One bird flies past—
A fan's
Fiber, shadows of wings
Dissolve into fearful seasweep.
Your sleeves,
For early spring's tomb,
Break and fall, suggesting
A certain birth.
At first it is the newly mounted *splash-ink*
Soon
Changes into an angry yet sorrowful
Knight rushing towards me.

Yeh Shan

WOUNDS: A SONG

You have never supposed you would
Live in that city.
Some bridges, some dead spirits'
Rags and remains. O will-o'-the-wisp!
A bee-raising, flower-growing brewery.
And we meet again, weep at
Cars and torrential rain flash by.

Because these are only odors and gestures.
Some strange blending, exuding from dust:
Mirror   dust   mirror   dust
Burning you within the reflected sadness, leaping into
Fresh flower's palm and treads.   Until yourself
Like plants in pieces and rotting.
You see yourself undress in stream's nostalgia
Undress and sink.   Scattering images—
These are not scales, nor hairs, nor annual rings felled.
Sudden flare of an evening, supposition of night.

YA HSIEN (WANG CH'ING-LIN), 1932–.

b.   Honan Province.

Major in the Chinese Navy, teaching dramatic arts at the Political Cadre Academy and National College of Fine Arts; spent 1965–67 in the Iowa International Writing Program; editor of the *Epoch Poetry Quarterly* (with Chang Mo and Lo Fu) and the *Young Lion Monthly*.

Poetry: *Selected Poems* (also entitled *One Night In Kúlinglin*, 1959)
        Salt (1968)
        Abyss (1968)

Statement:

Sometimes I think: A modern poet is not only a man of aesthetics, but also a *man* in the real sense of the word . . . he is a man in whose veins all kinds of desires roar. He pursues, gets lost, gets tired, and becomes furious. An hour ago, he might be seen with head hanging, comtemplating the growth of a blade of grass; an hour later, he might be seen in a low bar dipping his beard in a long-stemmed wineglass.

He tries to feel fully the life that can be felt. He clutches at it and on the third day when he becomes sober from over-drunkenness tries to render it in a hurry into something characterized by line divisions.

In one single poem, I am constantly trying to get into it what it is not usually expected to contain, so that it can comprehend all the complexities in human existence, from the Ultimate to love, death, spiritual quests, disillusions, fear, anxiety, hollowness and despair—in one sentence, I want to gulp down all the complex variegation in one's sensibility—I become so covetous that I can hardly get at a focus. And this intention gives birth to my *Abyss*.

————from "The Poet's Notebook"

Note: Poems with an asterisk were slightly reworded by Ya Hsien when he visited Iowa in 1965 and published them in his volume *Salt* (Iowa City, 1968).

Ya Hsien

SALT

Our old woman had never met Dostoevsky after all. In the spring
     she only cried: Salt! Give me a peck of salt! The angels were
     singing in the elms. That year the garden peas scarcely blossomed.

Seven hundred miles away the camel caravans led by the Minister of
     Salt were passing along the seaside. No blade of seaweed ever
     showed up in our old woman's pupils. She only cried: Salt!
     Salt! Give me a peck of salt! The laughing angels covered her
     up with a shower of snow.

In 1911 the partymen arrived in Wu-chang. Our old woman left her
     foot-binding cloth up on the elms and went off into the breath
     of wild dogs and under the wings of the bald-headed vulture.
     Many voices whined in the winds: Salt! Salt! Give me a peck
     of salt! Almost all the garden peas blossomed with white flowers
     that year. After all Dostoevsky had never met our old woman.

ON STREETS OF CHINA*

The blotting paper of dreams and moons.
Poets put on suits of corduroy.
The public telephones cannot be connected to the celestial Nü Wo.[1]
Thoughts walk on roads like scripts on oracle bones.
To feast on cooked wheat in an immense cauldron with the Muse.
Sandwiches and beef steaks are thus left unattended.
Poets put on suits of corduroy.

In the dust, Huangti,[2] our first emperor, shouts.
The trolley buses have left our Queen's phaeton rusted.
Since they have gaslights and neonlights,
We will not lend them our old old sun.

[1] Nü Wo, the legendary imperial lady (2738? B.C.) who attempted to repair the
cracks of the firmament with pieces of rocks.
[2] Huangti, the first emperor in China (2698? B.C.).

Recall, the greatest battle with Tzu-yu,[3] Huangti's enemy.
Recall, the Song of Reeling Silk sung by Lei-chu, Huangti's queen.[4]
Recall, that poets did not put on suits of corduroy.

No congress meetings and nothing had ever really happened.
Confucius had never imposed royalties on books by Laotze.
Airplanes roar and pass by a row of smoke-shrouded willows.
The tides of students' strikes dash on the eroded palace walls.
Without coffee without ever initiating a revolution, Li Po wrote his poetry,
Not to mention his not having to put on suits of corduroy.

Unexpectedly Whitman's collection did not come from Tun-huang.[5]
Oceanliners say: Beyond the four seas there are another four seas.
A beggar in the subway stretches out his black bowl.
Sailors flirt with girls scantily dressed.
And toward the left: red lights, and toward the right: red lights.
And poets put on suits of corduroy.

The advertisement of quinine is pasted on the face of our Husbandry
    Master.[6]
When spring comes, everyone is busy talking about interplanetary trips.
Steam whistles strangle the workmen. Pamphlets on democracy.
Bus stops. Lawyers and electric chairs.
On the gates of the city you will see no more heads hanging as deterrents.
Fu Hsi's Eight Diagrams [7] cannot catch up with the Nobel prizes.
The cypress in Confucius' hometown is made into railway ties.
If you want to put on anything, put on suits of corduroy.

[3] The battle between Huangti and Tzu-yu was said to be the greatest ancient battle, during which Huangti invented the first compass in the world.

[4] Lei-chu, Huangti's queen, who first discovered the use of silk.

[5] Tun-huang, a district in northwest Kansu province, noted for its priceless murals done in the T'ang Dynasty, and thus, the symbol of great culture.

[6] Husbandry Master or Shen Nung, a legendary emperor (2838? B.C.), who first discovered the use of herb medicine.

[7] Fu Hsi, brother of Nü Wo, a legendary emperor (2852?–2738? B.C.), famous for his invention of the Eight Trigrams, the first mystic form of prophetic expression which later developed into writing. He was also the first who taught the people to have their food cooked.

(All the above names are proverbial to the Chinese people.)

The blotting paper of dreams and moons.
Poets put on suits of corduroy.
People say there has never been such a creature as the dragon.
So feast on cooked wheat in an immense cauldron with the Muse.
So thoughts walk on roads like scripts on oracle bones.
And wait for the people coming out at the end of all sexy movies.
And put on suits of corduroy.

ANATOMY

There once was a man
Who was as truly thin as Jesus Christ
And longed to be nailed without mercy
(So that he might become famous)
And blood on his robe was splashed
And on his vulgar forehead that had been
Laughed at by the Philistines fell
A crown of thorns—only of paper glued together!
     But the price of the poplar was shooting up!
And nails have gone into the skyscrapers,
And people have almost lost the desire
To be Pharisees
Or to be St. Simeon;
To spit oaths on his not quite arched nose
Or to bear for him
The second ridiculous Cross.
     There once was a man
Who thought of these things after the sun had set.

LOYANG. 1942. IN TIME OF WAR

After springtime
Incendiary bombs held up the main street like a fan.
On the burnt chair
Of red sandalwood
My mother's hard smile rose to become a souvenir.

Thin-legged bees made their hives in the Seven-Mile Shrine.
My mother was half-drowned in the many
Dove-gray deaths last year,
And when the world did and re-did the same thing,
Her shoulder was made of stone,

That night between remorse and drowsing
A donkey brayed and brayed and a regiment of soldiers
Went down before the light poles beneath the windows
To spread out their papers.
The leaves of the Stone-Wood were so thick:
It was said nobody could sleep.

Yet from beginning to end
What they wanted was but to force you to choose a river;
To make you find a denouement,
Or write a long letter to your slim mistress in a neighboring village,
Or startle at a field of buckwheat.

But all these were done
The people were too tired to wait and expect and after all you had
        to participate
In the making of grass amid the buzzing of death;
And even—
Angels were no longer necessary.

ONE NIGHT AT KÚLINGLIN [1]

Little mother, please burn these aniseeds.
Little mother, please give me your blood.

Let me, too, become you for one night.
When dews cry desperately at the window,
Jesus will not be able to see us

[1] Kúlinglin is a small town near Taipei.

I will use my hair to cover—
Cover your naked body,
Like clothes, to free you from more pain.

Meanwhile, envy
        murmur
                concerning other weeds.
When an evening star suddenly appears,
Thriving under street-lamps
        Blocking pedestrians
Are these clamoring weeds,
That sense of danger,
        Even mowers abhor,
That danger of senses.

It is thus,
In the col between pillows,
Like two sea beasts cooling themselves,
Allowing their souls at their tongue's tip
Foul, strangle, stick together
And cause each other's death with liquid poison.
        (Dawn: we will hear no more
        Landlady's steps down the stairs. . . .)

Then we go, along the river;
Put on a cap to hide your earrings
To be my younger brother;
Bring me to see tides, flowers;
Go again, along the river,
Past this night, this star,
This dark beauty,
Past this bedsheet:
Bedsheet is our kingdom.

Little mother, let me give you my name.
Little mother, please give me your name.

Ya Hsien

LONDON

O Virginia!
In the night behind Westminster Abbey
When grey doves peck at the cracked bell
I am startled from sleep by your fierce tenderness.

Imagine now at the corner of the square
A gas lamp bearing the dark night.
A beggar beneath the corridor. Stars beyond the sky.
A chrysanthemum at the window. A sword in ancient times.

My Virginia is on the bed
Chewing a man's beard.
When her bracelet falls and the cedar wood murmurs
Between the mattresses there is a slight earthquake.

Your hair is the Congo
A horrible tributary.
Your arm has the stubbornness of a magnetic field.
Your eyes are rotten leaves, your blood goes naked.

And when the barefooted Jesus goes through the thick fog
To pawn his one bloody robe
I can clutch at nothing
Nothing but your brown-shaded breasts.

This is night, in the lower Thames,
The Thorn-Flower of your lips still grumbles at my cowardice in plucking,
A beggar beneath the corridor. Stars beyond the sky.
A chrysanthemum at the window. A sword in ancient times.

O Virginia! Before six we will be dead
When all London hides itself under a wig
Waiting for the food tray carried by a colored slave.
Even the sowing of pennies can harvest wheat.

Ya Hsien

A MORNING
(On the terrace)

In the morning
When the earth reveals in a Chinese chrysanthemum
A patch of the American sky,
I then remember
Yesterday. Yesterday, the name I used.

Through the purple-brown of the passage:
Girls sun on pomegranate trees
Their grass-like
       humid soul
While the mill of a neighbor's old gramophone
       (Offenbach driving an ass)
Begins, too, grinding some old dried corn.

In this way I remember
The name I used
The day before the day before yesterday,
Facing the sea, sitting on the terrace, wearing velvet pajamas,
And folding the love you gave me like an autumn fan
And trying to make myself go back
       To the patterns on a silver key's handle
       To such a classical fashion.

And this is morning
When the earth reveals in a patch of American sky
A little Chinese chrysanthemum.
Reading the papers from the capital,
I suddenly feel that for a long time God has not been here.

THAT WOMAN

That woman,
Behind her back wagging the streets of Florence,
Comes toward us like a portrait.

If I should kiss her
The oil paints of Raphael would certainly stick
On this exotic mustache of mine.

PROFESSOR C

In June his stiff white collar still supported his classical manner.
Every morning he tied his tie with a pre-War gesture;
Then, picking up a stick, a snuffbox, he went out
And when he passed the campus, there sprouted in him
The desire he had had in his earlier years
To be a statue.

But taking spinach for food was futile;
The zone beyond the clouds had long proved to be nothing.
When all the darkness bent itself down to grope for a lamp
He said he had had an immense face in the night
Composed of stars.

COLONEL

Purity was another kind of rose
Born of flames.
In the buckwheat field they encountered the greatest battle;
One leg said good-bye to him in 1942.

He has heard of history and laughter.

What, then, is immortal?
Cough syrups, razors, last month's rent and so on.
And beneath the snip-snap of his wife's sewing machine,
He feels the only thing capable of taking him captive is
The sun.

THE LATE GOVERNOR

When the bell struck seven his forehead and all his highness
Were professed crumbling
In the night borrowed from doctors
Beneath his sad but rich skin—

The chorus stopped abruptly.

Bustling among deaths of lime
Heaped up and heaped up
He would not have one bit of phosphorous more than the others,
                                                        Amen.

A NUN

Often she seemed to hear something, something calling her from afar
In a mackerel-colored afternoon.
When she had finished telling her rosary
She seemed to hear something.
And the sea lay beside the dock of ferry boats.
And it was in the afternoon as she was sitting,
The trumpet from the barracks went on sounding the same old tone,
As she was sitting.

There will be wind tonight, outside the wall a mandolin
Whining sadly sadly on its way—
"So was it once written in a book
And what has happened to the hero afterwards?"

Thus thinking to herself she was distracted . . .
She closed her eyes to rely on this one-minute night
And incidentally moved away the carnation on the piano
Because it made her heart ache.

TO R. G.

Along the waterside are a good many thick-lipped women.
They quarrel, using every possible shade
Of color. Autumn pushes away the clock face to create another glory
From the gloom of their hair.

This aimless smile rises continually and stops in the stars.

Melons and other fruits are laid
By the side of this composition.
It is the intolerable fouling of light after noontide,
One foot is arranged among wild fennels, another
Skulks away into the river.

On the four walls eyes are planted,
Glittering plots of land,
And the half leftover song is still held
By the slanting
Lyre.

The pallid flesh is forced to an original obedience
In this single-windowed
Rectangular night.

There is the handsome man, handsome R. G.

Good days when our friends are all carefree.
And death is not a parenthesis.
There is the handsome man, handsome R. G.

SETTING OUT

We have already weighed anchor. Under the brassy
Mortal and immortal sun
In the originally angel-less winds
The sea, blue for itself to see.

Ya Hsien

Tight between the teeth is
The shadow of mast and cordage.
Go to the rudder to see, in the wake, days of sweet seventeen,
And foot sigh's entire length on the deck, sitting
On the carpet she laid for me with her smile in days gone by,
Musing on an afternoon.

In Havana tonight some sort of murder is being held! Threats
Are finding house numbers. Gray bats fly round and round behind the city
　　　hall,
The piano plaintively whirls out a black umbrella.

　　　　　　　　　　　　　(What a pitiable sight! Her sleep
　　　　　　　　　　　　　Between endives and hill haws.)

They have (more bustling than the largest bazaar)
　　　　　　days of faces
　　　　　　days of postmen
　　　　　　days of streets
　　　　　　days of desperation and desperation.
On the immense vessel that will eventually sink into the soil
They clamor, with voices of eyes devoid of reasoning;
They hold their linen nervous system and forget the scissors . . . .

They are
Taking this tragedy
So appropriately.
It makes me happy.
I stand to port, giving my necktie to the wind, and smile.

ABYSS *

Children often get lost in your curls.
The earliest torrent of spring lurks behind your savage pupils.
One part of the year is crying out. Flesh makes a festival of the night,
In the virulent moonlight, in the delta of blood,

All the souls coiled together strike at
The downcast forehead hanging on the Cross.

This is absurd. In Spain
Nobody will throw him a second-rate wedding cake!
And we put on mourning for everything; it takes a whole morning merely
                                        to touch the hem of his cloak.
Afterwards his name is written on wind, on flags.
Afterwards he tosses us
The leftover life he's been eating.

To go and see, to pretend to be sad, to smell the decay of Time.
We are once more too lazy to know who we are.
Work. Promenade. Salute the badmen. Smile and become immortal.
They are the ones who hold onto maxims!
This is the countenance of days: all wounds groan; bacteria haunt skirts.
Metropolis. Scales. Paper-moon. The language of electric poles.
(Today's posters pasted on yesterday's.)
The cold-blooded sun goes on trembling
In the narrow abyss
Between two nights.

Years, cat-face years,
Years that stick close to the wrist, years that wag semaphore flags.
In the rat-weeping nights, the killed are being killed again.
They make bow ties with graveyard weeds and grind the Lord's Prayer
                                        between their teeth.
No head can really rise among the stars,
Or wash a crown of thorns in the glittering blood;
In the 13th month of the 5th season of the year, heaven lies down below.

We erect a tombstone for last year's moth; we are living.
We cook wheat with barbed wire; we are living.
Through the sad rhythm of billboards, through the filthy shadow of cement,
Through the souls released from the prison of the ribs,
Hallelujah! we are living. Walk, cough, argue,
Stiffen your face to occupy part of the world.

Ya Hsien

There is nothing, the now is dying.
Today's clouds copy yesterday's.

In March I hear the hawking of the cherry.
With the shaking of many tongues spring declines; the bottle flies
                                        are biting her face:
The slits of the *ch'i-p'ao* swing between certain legs; longing to be read
And entered and worked. And except for death and this
There is nothing definite. Being is wind; being is the noise of the thrasher;
Being is—to those who like to be tickled—
To pour out the whole summer of desire.

At night everywhere beds are falling. The sound of a beam of fever-
                                        stricken
Light walking on shreds of glass. The forced, blind disorder of farming tools.
The scandalous translation of flesh. A terrifying language
Spelled out in kisses. The first acquaintance of blood and blood,
                                        a flame, a fatigue!
The gesture of ferociously pushing her away.
At night, in Naples, everywhere beds are falling.
At the end of my shadow there sits a woman, weeping.
The baby is interred between snakeroot and tiger lily . . .
The next day we go together to look at the clouds, smile and drink
                                        plum juice,
And dance and dance the last of our manhood away in the dance hall.
Hallelujah! We are still living, our head is still on our shoulders;
Holding up our being and not-being:
Holding up a caught-in-the-act face.

Next chapter. On whom? Maybe on a churchmouse, maybe on the look
                                        of the weather.
We bid farewell far far away to the long-long-hated umbilical cord.
Kisses hanging on our lips, religion imprinted on our face,
We loaf about, carrying our own coffin lid on our back.
And you are the wind, the bird, the look of weather, the river without
                                        a mouth,
The corpse-ash standing, the uninterred death.

Nobody will pluck us out of the earth. To see life with closed eyes.
Jesus, do you hear the rustling of a jungle growing in his brain?
A flogging is heard beneath the beet field, under the myrtle is . . .
When some countenances change like a lizard, how can a torrent fashion
an image
Of the upsidedown? When their eyeballs are pasted
On the darkest pages of history?

And you are nothing;
Not he who breaks his stick on the face of the Age,
Nor he who turbans aurora on his head and dances.
In the shoulderless city, your book will be pounded into paper pulp
on the third day.
You wash your face with the night; you duel with your shadow;
You come out from the house and go in and rub your hands . . .
You are nothing.

Just how are you to increase the strength of a flea's leg?
To inject music into the throat and make the blind drink up the brightness!
To sow seeds on the palm, to milk moonlight from the breasts!
—In this night which rotates round and round you, there you have a share,
Coquettish and beautiful, these are yours:
A flower, a bottle of wine, a bed of pleasure, a date.

This is the abyss, between the bedclothes, pale as funeral scrolls!
There, the oval-faced sisters, and there, the window, the mirror, the
little puff box.
This is smiling; this is blood; this is the ribbon waiting to be untied!
That night there was left on the wall only the picture frame of the
Maria; she had run away,
Seeking for Lethe to wash away the shameful things she had heard.
And this is an old story, old as a revolving lantern;[1] O organ organ organ!
When in the morning I take up a basketful of sins and go out hawking on
the streets,
The sun pricks my eyes with the wheat's beard.

Hallelujah! I am still living.
Work. Promenade. Salute the badmen. Smile and become immortal.

Ya Hsien

To live for the sake of living, to gaze at clouds for the sake of gazing
at them.

Stiffen your face to occupy part of the world . . .
By the side of the Congo River, there a sled stops;
Nobody knows how it could have slid so far,
The sled nobody knows stops there.

EASTER DAY

She walks south along Te-hui Street.
After September she does not seem to like
The man she loved before the war.
The rest we are not familiar with.

Or river or star or night
Or bouquets or guitar or spring
Or who should be responsible for a certain mistake, the not quite definite,
          mistake
Or something else.

And all these hardly form a song.
Although she walks south along Te-hui Street
And suddenly raising her head
Sees, in a flash, a whole row of tooth-paste ads.

[1] A kind of Chinese lantern within a lantern: as it burns, the inner lantern revolves, showing usually a pattern of horses running.

PAI CH'IU (HO CHIN-JUNG), 1937–.

b.   Taiwan Province.

Furniture designer; editor of *Li* (poetry magazine).

Poetry: *The Death of a Moth* (1959)
         The Wind-Rose (1965)
         Sky Symbolism (1969)

Statement:

The first prerequisite for a poet is to live truthfully, to feel life in its difficult aspects, to understand the solitude of the individual in the human situation with a transcendental perspective. Poetry is the record of the poet's quest in the absolute solitude of life.

Art is great before our eyes because the technique with which it is presented is great. The second prerequisite is, therefore, to remold, as in the fashioning of a handful of clay, and to reorganize into a new mode all the words, ancient and modern, and their combinations that he employs in his poetry.

The existing forms of beauty become a pressure upon and trial for the beauty yet to appear. If we cannot break through this barrier and transcend it, it will be quite impossible for new forms of beauty to emerge. And the poet concerned with this artistic principle will always consider his last poem or the poem still in his mind the most finished expression.

——from the "Postscript" to *The Death of a Moth*

WANDERER
(A concrete poem)

Pai Ch'iu

```
look-
ing
into
the
dis-       look-
tance      ing                                          a
toward     toward                                       sil
a          a          a                                 ken
cloud-     cloud-     cloud-                             pine
like       like       like                              t
silken     silken     silken     silken                 r
pine       pine       pine       pine                   e
tree       tree       tree       tree     on the horizon  e     on the horizon
```

A Note on Concrete Poetry

  Concrete poetry, such as *Wanderer*, is a simple maneuver for a Chinese poet, because many of the characters with which he writes his poem still retain a recognizable pictorial base. (One must reassert here that the pictorial quality of the Chinese character *does exist,* in spite of the denial made by some sinologists.) This quality can be, and has been, exploited for richer poetic textures. Apart from their inherent pictorial possibilities, the Chinese characters are equal in size, square in shape (although the calligrapher may vary them for plastic reasons, they are always maintained in the same size in writing and printing) and free from fetters of grammar (tense declensions, in particular), making it extremely flexible for the poet to juggle them around to design poems of shapes and poems of spatial feeling.

```
his        he         stand

shadow     has

small      for-                  stand-

his        gotten                ing                                            a

shadow     his                                                                 lo

small      name                  stand-                            EAST.       ne

           for-                  ing                        the                sil

           gotten                                   ward                       ken

           his                   standing       to-                           pine

           name       but        standing                                     t

           he         stand                                                    r

           can        a-                                                       e

           but        lone                                                     e
```

Since it is relatively easy for a Chinese poet to manipulate these inherent qualities, concrete poetry has not attracted too many devotees, although they all welcome new possibilities in this genre. A few Chinese poets, however, making the most of the Chinese characters, have produced some very successful poems. But, as we all know, concrete poetry is not to be translated; it is to be read and/or viewed *as is*. Accordingly, I have omitted in this anthology the few poets whose uniqueness seems to lie in this genre at this writing, among them Lin Heng-t'ai and Fang Hsin, although the latter also wrote in other forms. Risking a translation of the form as I am now, I have ventured the above experiment to reproduce the effect of Pai Ch'iu's poem as an epitome of one small segment of modern Chinese poetry.

Pai Ch'iu

ON THE TERRACE

You won't understand how your name was gone. On the terrace, the cat-shaped cinnabar cloud, in the deportment of a wolf-dog, brushes by the Parisian sky lurking behind a young girl's pupils, and with various gestures looks over you—that island beyond the sea, sea beyond island, island beyond sea and sea beyond island. Surely, you won't understand how your name was gone.

O no love in love and love in no love—how contradictory yet how simple an existence in a dewdrop in the Great Limit and the Great Limit in a dewdrop, etc., and etc. . . . Surely, you won't understand how your name was gone in my heart.

AUTUMN

On the face identical every year, as if
We have lived thousands of years of love, autumn
Remains the way autumn has been. Those
Bean-sprout faces chased after by the wheel of war
We are like a fresh fish starting to rot
Rotting rotting rotting rotting rotting

In the world's pool, the low-clouded sky from afar
Is like the loaded belly of a short-breathed pregnant woman
Every year the identical face. Many thousand years we lived.
Ai! those iron-shoes take turns to ravish our wife of hope!

We are a deserted roadside house looking
Emptily at the road in front of the door
                              disappearing into the distance

POEM

I

Like a moon you wheel across my lake-heart
I do not remember when it was
In a night solitary and silent like this
I looked for you, kneeling down to touch you with my hands
With eyes of a thousand "firefly-lamps"
With the breath of unbroken spring winds

But you have been only a formless light
Under this arched heaven of sounds
Where there is no voice, yet echoing constantly
There are no eyes, yet staring constantly
Like a dream
Which is ubiquitous in time and space

Like a moon you wheel across my lake-heart

II

Nothing on which to rely
Singly
The solitude of a man
Becomes a sea
Swallowing me

O
Night is hollow and void
Letting loose my virgin heart
As night withers
    Drooping, its petals

Because night is like flower
I am like flower
Virgin heart is like flower

III

Although you should let open the door of desiring something
This

Has nothing to do with me. Let
The sky be blue frankly
Let the wind be itself among pines
For this bright bright bright world

And I myself wither
Becoming a deserted path of a thousand years
Becoming a discolored pansy
A sentence of beaten confession . . .

IV

The hand that knocked at the door returns no more
The hand that knocked at the door returns no more
There was someone . . .
But I wither like the flower-heart, wither at your singing
Beyond the brilliance of varied lights

O let memory be like the wind:
There was once walking through wheat fields, rustling
                    waves dashing and roaring
There was an ancient bell muted

But now all sounds turn into songs, forming a stretch
Of oozing water, but I am only
A lotus failing to clutch at anything to stay . . .

V

The era of impossible wars. We
Write poetry like stitches of embroidery
The dancing feet on the waxed floor
The music that slices into knots our drowsiness. In spring

Mothers do not go up the tower to look, but
Steal from the sons' pockets and go out secretly
To quarrel at Mahjong tables. Heroic fathers
Busy building dens.

Only those slack and listless winds
The sickening flowering Chinese phoenix
Only those slack and listless winds

WIND-ROSE

Let silence
Lie on midnight streets
Sudden, nerve-breaking horns cut past
Like a freshly sharpened drill
Then blood, dreary red
Hopelessly flows down

1

Standing, I am life in the winds
Standing
Reluctantly standing
Doomed
To be a rose
And reluctantly standing:
Here.

No venting of feelings
My words are
Blown by winds
Nothing to lean on
My overcoat
Is only boring time

No eyes
To gaze at your creation
There are loudening waves against the distance
No ears

2

When all the eyes in the night sky
Gaze at me
No love
Such hollow
Will
I open myself
Like curtains

Only a dark cold
Room
A bodiless
Shirt

3

No thanksgiving, facing
You and sunshine
Giving me water
Knowledge and history

I am but
Parents' pleasure's
By-product
No character
Only to stand here
Only to go on being
A rose
And standing here

Unable to bestride a step

4

Other roses
Other roses
Other roses
Only roses
Only roses
Only roses
All roses
All roses
All roses
Everything, roses
Everything, roses
Everything, roses
Everything, roses

Pitiful! I am too a rose

5

Existence is not philosophy
—Dark-crystal surface of water
Wind's footfalls pass by
Even though
Millions of reflections
Spy

Your name
Is only ripples on water
Existence
Is only existence

6

Within
Cities die
All doors
Disorderly open, unable

To find a face
No
Flow of language

All branches
Become unconscious hand gestures
Moon is only cutout silver paper
No response

I am only
A hollow rose

7

Because space is overly vast
And becomes trembling, freedom
Creates
Our solitude

Among ongoing incoming waves, will
Is refuse
Even to go ahead is not future
Choice and circumstances
In conflict
Direction, only a probability
Time gives us only one road
Look ahead go ahead
We know no conclusion

Gods die in freedom
Gods die in space
We reluctantly choose
To express a shred of will

8

Maria
As in beri-beri

Greets, makes your
Sighs overflow from the cup
Clean-white and soft
Swan to me is also
Like a white wall, an indifferent
Face

On this land of sands
My existence is already ironical
Don't sing
Your song
Your nursery rhyme

WIFE'S BELLY

Harken: in the dark room of night
Seeds waking up yawn and stretch
With knock knock upon the door

ROADS, A THOUSAND PIKES; TREES, A THOUSAND ROOTS
(In memory of my dead parents)

Roads: a thousand pikes, pikes calling to me
Trees: a thousand roots, roots calling to me

But the roads leading here
Are buried in the wind-blown sand
Life-beginning roots
Are rotten

This bustling world
Has left behind but one *me*

one.

Pai Ch'iu

DIE WITH THE WHITE GLARE

Streets beyond the sill, shot, struggled and sank. Night
Comes and throws palls on them. Dew
Wets our open eyes.
For the shrill, grass-like soul,
In the midway,
We, alone, against nothing, die a blank, blank death.

Because of us, winds speed away in all directions.
Bodies are now like gun-smashed, deserted markets.
We have no place to hide. Tomorrow
The poppy will cover us beautifully.
We will band together with wandering spirits
And go out begging everywhere.

Eye-sockets will be eroded by darkness into two deep wells
To hold, for thousands of years, only cold rain.
And on the darkened road of no distance, we hand our eyes
Over to stars to shine on our wandering bodies' shadows.

YIP WAI-LIM (YEH WEI-LIEN), 1937–.

b.   Kwangtung Province.

Co-editor at different times of *New Currents, Modern Literature* and the *Epoch Poetry Quarterly;* spent 1963–64 in the Poetry Workshop, The University of Iowa; Ph.D. in comparative literature from Princeton University in 1967, and since then has been teaching Poetics, English and Chinese Poetry, as well as Poetry Workshop in the Department of Literature, University of California at San Diego.

Poetry: *Fugue* (1963)
   Collected Poems (1969)

Statement:

The monotonous engine has smoothed out the breath of the sleeping passengers on the plane. The sun is not yet up. Clouds fly noiselessly outside the window. Perhaps because of this absolute silence, just as all the activities down below are arrested by the deep winter snow, one passenger, who is not sleeping, unconsciously becomes silence itself and hears the sound of snow falling, the sound of the movement of the sun, which is not yet here but which is on its way; and the blooming of flowers, which are now still in hibernation but which will wake up in spring. Limits of space and limits of time do not exist in the consciousness of this passenger. He has *another hearing, another vision.* He hears voices we normally do not hear. He sees activities across a space not to be seen by the physical eye. Nor is the passenger conscious of any linear, causal developments between or among these things . . . and prose is a linear structure defined by limits of space and time, so this passenger writes a poem.

Yip Wai-lim

DESCENDING
(Selections)

III. *Every Day Mountains Rise and Fall from Our Shoulders*

Every day mountains rise and fall from our shoulders and
Like great wings of care-directing sea currents
The far-pouring sun of mercury
Directs radiations of our dreams. The conch of Death
Blows for many sumptuous weddings of yesterday. Tempests silently lead
The eagle of our desire to circle above the lines of earth's palm
     Heads of curiosity and sickness: a torrent of falling stones
     Run into the all-reaching long long streets
     The gibble-gabble of women and children in the afternoons
     Reveals new deities
     The transient beds
     Point out every day our confine

     (We no longer see the woman's offering of breasts in her hands)

And then, dear Exile of Exiles, we discarded all our ice-winged ships
to keep night watches on our way through quicksand; and then we
burnt all the hubbub of cities and arose; and then we were flags,
flags without the festivities of *Ch'ing-ming* and *Ch'ung-yang*.

Every day the white fungoid sun stays on earth's mercury
Every day the eagle of our desire pecks the rising winds and
When the highland is stretched by the fires of evening
You will find me and my horse standing there

IV. *Crawling Out From Our Fingers* . . .

Crawling out from our fingers, you at once commanded
The monstrous age and weather. Emerging from water the ships commanded
The port of bone ashes and tombstones. Brother, how your clamorous
                                   wagon-theatre
Went into the prison of singing and drank the rising sands of the horizon

And at the turn of a broken wall you found yourself eating lime fruits
                                                     and flowers
After the avalanche that alarmed the villagers, how you became
The vocabulary of our desire and the flawless virgins of the rock took off
All their draping to face the persisting blue—
What can be compared to this persisting blue?
And the flawless virgins of the rock took off all the rigs of steel
And began their great mastless voyage under the eaves
Brother, when a woman falls asleep on your shoulder, does she
Know that the drama of your tremendous robe has already commanded
All ages and weathers, does she know that night
You, holding a lamp, saw me out of those happy steps to look for
The sacrificed moon and the burnt stars and to sea-bury
The woman of the land?
Brother, when the flawless virgins of the rock took off all their draping
Had you fallen into this persisting blue?

ARE SUCH THE VOICES . . .

Are such the voices we never heard, O you dumbfounded season
Voices of falling, voices of shining and blooming?
Are you the rising that doubles the sea and the sky
And lets the yearlong hair of clouds stir
The conflagration of the ancient hoofs
From the white-erosive flood?
Where, one may ask, does the song end?
Among the blue, blue hills?
And where, the yellow birds' way?
Where, the sea-gulls' flight?
When all colors are now governed by one
When all voices stay in your face
The cities in the horizon disperse and cliffs sink
The tremendous flapping now strikes the void
As the stone head that is never given the seven apertures
Commands the growing picture of our knowledge
What swelling movements from flowers

Which defy shaping and naming
That have made everything explainable?
We suddenly see so many door handles
That lead us to courts and bowers
Where you, rising once again, with postures of a relief
So stun us that we have to resist
Rivers, forests and villages from being washed away
And the longing of soldiers on the only towers
From dissolving into a season, dissolving
Into the soundless roaring of a fall
When the paths of woodcutters
Slowly and silently
Reach the yearlong clouds

ENORMOUS STILLNESS . . .

Enormous stillness . . . a tract
of watery sensations drift
on the floor
Autumn falls abruptly from the eaves
As syllables of voices flame
out of the uncouth chambers of the heart
The enveloping night mystifies
the eye and the visible
Autumn falls.
The room sinks into a trance in brew
Rustling of silk gliding over strings of a lute
So we go into a rainy season
Rains that have a downward cadence
downward down-a-down
In the faraway provinces
a shower slashes a city in an afterglow
stirs up a flight of white cranes
from the marshes
In an afterglow they say one senses

a pavilion of brightness of the past
screened in a sunny shower
undertones in time of war
gold winds winding down the cornfield
wafting a flowing of glimmering hair
with a downward cadence
downward down-a-down
A canticle of bones
rises
Drums and heads of martyrs from the plain
flow here and away
with a downward cadence
downward down-a-down

(Unknowing of full dawn's advent.   That comes like the wheel
Comes in mourning drapery.   Where the door opens
The shouting of peddlers of the well-known yesterday.)

FUGUE

I

North wind   can I bear this one more year?
Streets shivering along the walls
Romances in cold sorrows from the frontiers
Remind me of these:
Patience of mountains   Erratic breath of outlands
Chronic neighing of Tartar horses
Bonfires in war and farming in spring
Plants that transcend all knowing
Immaculate snowfalls   Grand cathedrals and palaces
All plunge into the scandals of gods
That follow our youthful days
The song goes:
        The moon will rise
        The sun will sink

Please be quick   And do not get lost in the sun
Have you forgotten the oracle of the dragon?
It may slip again from the jade balcony
Into this only aspen among
Compacted houses   Yesterday
Or today? (I am not yet sure)
Beside the river or the deep-flowing water
                         or the dark-shimmering rushes
I see a cloud of crows gather around a drifting of lives
                                   But where to?
The winds bring the barking of dogs into winding back alleys
The poets are dead   The Vixen comes in silk
Is the one-eyed seer still living?
The winds roar   In the cold streets in the flying dust
I can still recognize this is the bus to my native land
Tables mats and wines proudly invite me
To see the stars—fugitive ideas on flowers
And intentions in myths
                    We go sight-seeing

II

My feet my hands collide together   In the rushing coach
Stumps upheld the fleshy body of winter
In the rush the fire burns the lucent days of the past
In the rush the boulevard tempers the lucent days of the past
A line of thatched huts and flying birds embrace
My skyward solitude   I go in search of
Vespers and festivals within a tent   A beach
A kitten   rains in apricot days   and smoke from wild ferns
That occurred in the first frost shortly after my vigorous hands
Caressed a holy face
                He stood up
Imitating the ancient prophet:
                    By the Twelve Branches
                         It comes true
                         It comes true

I wait for you and bring you to see the dynasties of T'ang Yü Hsia
    Shang Chou

The earth holds wallowing memories
        the great book read into the world
        the child on stretching plains
        the giant of uprising ranges
The earth holds wallowing memories

Glimmering Mars strolls over our gardens
A man with disheveled hair sings:

                        I want to see the land of Lu
                        Mount Kuei hides it
                        And I have no axe or hatchet
                        What can I do to Mount Kuei?
Warm the southerly winds
Soothe our woes the southerly winds
Increase our gains the southerly winds
                    In early winter
                    In whispers
                    In sickbed

The fire burns the lucent days of the past
The boulevard tempers the lucent days of the past
We drink to the flowering chrysanthemum   make a flute from reeds
And play a stanza from the fugitive song

III

Do you not see people seek for their children
                        the embryo of man?
Do you not see people seek from sudden falls
                        an ode of stone?
Do you not see people seek in the jingling of spears
                        communion with the heavens?

Note: Lu, birthplace of Confucius, has been a synonym for the
    great culture in the past.

Against the maple the willow the wind and the wine of a poet
There is the speech of cliffs   the hurrah of the sea
The soundless pit of sky as we now remember
A spring turns into a pond
     or gets into plants
     or gets into human bodies
     regardless of reality
     regardless of the Great Void
We simply walk down the steps   No monsoon
Nor omened events coming on
We brood over a tale: A peach or a desire
Which spoils the moral of the celestial court? O how boring
Let me tell you the charm of a white mouse . . .
                         But on craggy precipices
Or on rocky ruins of a long wall
What can we make of the world?
                    We have ourselves admired
Millions of flowers trees bays and waters
What can we make of the world?
   We have again come across
Rimes meters rhythms tones ballads etc.
What can we make of the world?
Board a congested bus   stand beside the streets
Look here and there   wait for a butterfly
Wait for a supreme seer wait for a knight on horseback
Pass by
        How many faces
        How many names
Flouted by trees and buildings
        Longingly I think of my friends
        I stop and scratch my head
Night brings down a galaxy of chilling rain

LOOKING UP: A SONG
In a deserted station
A wrinkled Buddha wakes up . . .

Castoff memories uphold me and I stretch
Because only stretching is godly. I stretch
My white-winged longing to your custom-ridden clouds
And following the innocent river of winds
Repeat the story in the clean void bosom of an infant
You go into light just as a lion
Walks to the water brim. Sound enters you
When trees spread out and fan-shaped recordings
Move out of the long-winding wall
When the copious eyesight of the child
Suddenly among many forms standing in the plaza raises
A string of water-beads from bathing girls to welcome
And wide windows crowded with faces to hurrah
My far-going popular odyssey
Because cities and towns themselves rise
In full summer's scent of woodcutting
And God and famine become allusions one after the other
Amid the unanswering swaying of leaves among rooftrees
Because the child of the wind
Because the child of the cloud
    (Those are guests from gestures of flowers
    Those are ships from a face
    Those are blue from gazing
    Those are sugar
    From the look of mountains)
Because the child of the wind
Because the child of the cloud
My wooden horse on the waves
My bell in speech
When desires give birth to arrivals and departures
When fatigued forms press toward stations
When burning silence extinguishes boundaries
The child of the wind
The child of the cloud

Do you know how paddy fields are caught by new ears
How I by stories, how rivers by banks
Banks by wayfarers, wayfarers by
The maguey sun?
Flowers burst forth from the broken wall and I stretch
As only stretching is godly and I stretch
Toward ten miles, a million miles
Ten miles, a million miles of fear

WHITE DEATH

Uproar, ceramics,
Tier upon tier,
Tremble at the eyebrows.
Gold foils glimmer, burning,
The cream-colored castle.
Birdless, the sky blazes.
Immaculate hands
Thrust forth
From attenuated breath,
Like beaten flax
Against the brimming dawn.
Creaking of spindles,
Silent closing of doors
Are now childhood
Shut in brain's lobes.
Turbulent rocks
From star-white curtains
Attend the last wash
Of the nervous system.
In the wind, perhaps,
One can desire
To become wordless scenery,
Or green tiles
Relieved of flames.
Perhaps, waiting itself

Is a jade tree,
The primeval cold
Clotted in your eyes.
Winter refuses luxuriance.
Grottos define themselves
By being solid.
Mountains are made
to flow seaward.
No river can
Avoid lowlands.
No lake
Can uplift itself.
All cries,
Having left the lips,
Burst into flowers,
Dripping,
The white wounds of the sun.

Among sky-trailing frost-branches
Horses are running.
Beyond the clouds,
             blue, upon blue.

SAN FRANCISCO

The uddered sea guarded by angelic children
Bats of winds webbing white holes of desire
Last night or tonight when
All fruits of light roll down
To explode into new flowers
My feet rise into mid-darkness
Of welcoming hands that blind my way
The rattling black stars
From my growing sleep
Become the loins that fasten me
On my body of prenatal cyclone

(Clothes rustled by breath of pores)

The uddered sea guarded
Bats of winds webbing
The petrified blood on bluff of birth
From deck of dream a fleshed fault
Grows into an eternal flow
Of unedited editions of shipments
Schedules for circulations of mountains and rivers
Into gun barrels and water pipes
To make a gloomy day of angelic faces
Burnt by drums and horns
To make eyesight into a chain of rusty rings

(Clothes rustled by breath of pores)

The uddered sea guarded
Bats of winds webbing
San Francisco with his many arms
And star-starked stare
Wants to push open his bosom
To see tomorrow

THE WARM, WARM JOURNEY

I. Andante
You may be absorbed in gazing
Or at sea.
The garden gate may be wide open.
Yet no scenery moves in.
Upon the steps, peacocks cry.
Windowpanes sway back and forth,
Back and forth, the gold-black cups and glasses
In the porcelain sink,
As if the green pears upon the tree, too,
Resound the striking on the anvil.

Yes, whatever hour you rise from bed,
Whichever end of corridor you come out from,
On the long couch there always leans
The warm sleep wrapped up in white reeds.
The wall is an enclosure of thick fog
Kneading into void all the smell of burnt rubber
And the turning wheels in the midst of signs
Where all dark birds are dead.
Sleep wrapped up in warm white reeds,
Clouds gather around the clear singing.
All the stars and stones sunk in the sea
Now gather before the round window upon the cliff.
Yes, as you count the flying birds in the distant smoke
And listen to the tides from perforated bricks
Where you stand is the unfurling, hanging hair
And dianthus in big clusters upon the white-glazed vase:
"Please do not disturb the fluffy snob dog!"
When the song ends, all clouds break
                    "EXTRA! EXTRA!"
On the long couch there still lies
The warm, warm sleep wrapped up in white reeds.

II. Moderato

Sepals fall.
The rag of soot-smoke succumbs to sudden rain.
Beneath the bath, the watercourse guggles.
You come out from the calyx, wading through pungent days,
Stepping many selfsame steps among frames.
Suddenly waves bloom in full:
"How am I to sew my body
To my two legs?
How can the scattered crystal limbs
Become the scent after petals are cast off
Or the cohesive core of diamond
Upon the humming high-tension antenna?"
The conch scours algae and sands:

Splashing of oars. In the jade sky
The gauze nets the stopped dawn.
Caves net the sun.
    And clamoring birds cover the spring mountain.
What happens afterwards? The boat drifts left and right.
The keel combs kelps. Noiseless is the mountain fall.

Cloud-cutting petals fall into the watery street after rain.
A company bus happens to be passing by.

THE CROSSING

I

In the midst of talking,
              it comes:
        breaks knotted noises
        nips budding blooms
That year—attenuated desires
That year—scheme of sadness stretched:
Beneath the barquentine, jadelike water
Evening crows were gone with the surge
Wife said: Let us set sail
                eastward (It doesn't matter)
                westward (It doesn't matter)
Lingering house ashes blown
Into threads as from bobbins to weave
Noiselessly
The cloth of memory
Don't we have the cradle of the sea?
Let our boy Begonia's dream
Seep into the surf off starboard
In the midst of our talking
Wife's hair fluttered behind her
The thudding of war

Sleep, baby, sleep
Bright snow we keep
Fear no brides
Stepping, stepping up to you
Sleep, baby, sleep
No waking, no fright
Although King of Wounds are you

Sleeping,
     waterfall thunders from the dam
So distant, so faraway, as if
High-hanging intravenous feeding
Across the broken sundown
Ferrying troups of girls in white
Whose fingers draw
     a chord of land, mist-masked
       a man
Shakes an incensed bell, sprinkles
Gold waves on parched hands
When the crystal keel glides into the veins

   "The wind is up! Strike sail! Steer!"

Boom! Instead of quicksand, a clear lake
O King, why cry at the water's brim
For your Lady, your corteges?
Shoulder up your city:
Your sky-reaching footfalls are full
Of your Lady, your corteges
O King, grieve no more
Wherever you go, the city will be with you

II

Leisurely, catkins hover
In the limpid sun
A dove, mouthing a little cloud
Pierces the mountain road

You lean on the window sill
As if on your skirt
      (Darkly, sandalwood burns)
And float a paper-flower boat
Outside the window
         Checkered leopard's back
Up and down moves. And from you:
Winds circle behind Kings' Canyon
Like stars, white day and bird songs fall
Amid thick sound-blasts of the engine
A slanting big city blooms
Furrows and furrows of flowers
      Making night
      Like you
Lean on the skirt: crystal cold arms
Rimless gaze
As skating knives flash-flash cut into
The still, still circle
No other way. Thus, the King's reply:
Don't be sorrowful because you see no more
The torrential ocean
Leaning on the window sill
Let us hearken: swelling tides in the veins

III

Dear father:
      Fruits die in their taste and nourishment
      We say good-bye to fields and to work
      Door beyond door, gate beyond gate
      In a park, thunderous steps
      We loosen our hair into flags
      And—naked—sing:
            Corpulent circle, turn O turn
            You, outside the circle
            I, inside it
            Corpulent circle, turn O turn
            Circle turns into a dot

You and I sleep on a cot
Corpulent dot, turn O turn

Often up on the steeple, we unmoor the stars
And speed on the five-strings among cloud-trees
And think of the death of fruits in cabins
Night comes: all mountains rise
Drumsticks fall, water birds soar
We join hands to anchor one by one
By the sky-obscuring guitar's loins
And loosened hair flutters
                Fluttering hair is our Name

IV

Such a rare night of north wind
A thousand trees, a million trees of frost flowers
                (How lovely!)
A thousand trees, a million trees of frost flowers
              (Who's going to see?)
The portal is lost in a hanging shadow of sky
I stop to think: kingfisher after kingfisher
Pecks and pecks at the dripping color of spring
Because there was once you, O King
Once you: splash the Milky Way
        ride on singing
        break tree walls
When two banks of mountain flowers opened like clouds
Bells and drums joined
            and you said:
The fertile sun comes rumbling
Forests break, mountains end
We spray wine into mist
To find in it a hand
To pass a door
In a windless room, cock an ear
To a gushing fountain
To endless footfalls

O King, I hear only frost flowers crack
You walk away on the fragile nervous system
At the fort, you seemed to have said:
Give you my blood, give you Begonia

City walls drowned in the dawn
A thousand trees
A million trees
Of
Frost flowers
A thousand trees
A million trees
Of
Frost flowers
   When winds fall
   Spring grass grows lush:
   Begonia, O Begonia, where's my Begonia?

      V

Once there was a King
He walked among whistling poplars
Air gathered around him
He rushed toward trees among clouds
Cloud-trees carried sun's white shadow
Waves carried palls of satin
Our King, eyeless and lashless King
His trembling lips, what do they spell?

Once there was a King who had a son
Called Begonia. (The rest we can't tell)
Begonia rushed to skyward pillars
Leaned on an ash tree, watched gurgling springs
A white horse flashed between stone crevices
Air spread to earth-gray river
On it drifted a guitar of hair-pendants
Our Begonia
His open mouth, what does it sing?

Our King in the story had a wife
On the dam she saw water spray wash the sunset
Listened to Sisters in white ring beyond the surge
And doves coo on the sand
But pine clouds were so very nice
Flower not flower, leaves not leaves
She did not understand why a blast of wind
Blew Sister's black umbrella toward her
She'd rather it be a barquentine

Once there was a King who had a son
Called Begonia who had a mother
She walked on the impregnable bridgehead;
Seagulls combed buildings, night oppressed tides
Fishes, the river mouth; many hands wave windows
Whose singing so very pleasing
So very pleasing it was like an attentive Blue Bird
Flap-flap-flap in the white-glaring mulberry woods
Begonia's mother
Leaning on iron railings murmured, murmured
What is she calling for?

    Sleep, baby, sleep
    Please do not weep
    King has satin sheets
    Begonia has a white steed
    Sleep, baby, sleep
    No vigil to keep
    Pine-surges will look after wife
    Blue Bird will attend mother
    Harken:
        At the foothills
           fresh, sudden rains
        Down beneath, above streams
           clouds over clouds fly

HUANG YUNG 1936–.   用

b.   Fukien Province.

"Economist, table-tennis champion, biochemist," doing post-doctorate research at Washington University, St. Louis, Missouri.

Poetry: *Fruitless Flowers* (1959)

Statement:

In modern times, "eternity" has acquired a new definition. It is no longer the continuity of endless time, but extreme perfection and fullness. Poetry in modern times does not search for the inaccessible permanence and universality, it aims at the release of its character. . . .

——from the "Preface" to *Fruitless Flowers*

RAINY DAYS

A lover's white bones. A soggy road in the dusk
Leads away and back.

The gate of a garden.
A pale warrior back from the war
Knocks, like a stranger, knocks at his own closed doors.
The gardenful of weeds is more silent than in spring,
More dumb than the rusted door rings.
The world has been destroyed so many times
And this garden stays.

Genial rains, yet too cold.
Lines of silk falling, genial words.

Who gets the whipping?
In the dusk there is only the soggy road.

STANDING STILL IN A CASUAL MOMENT

Were it in Venice
I would be able to find a reason
        for several fishing lines flowing out from your window.
But so distant! O Mediterranean Sea.
                O Jerusalem.
And I am a pilgrim fish.

Far-off I see you
Smile
Like a monastery in a remote land
Where, when the wind comes, one sees the bells swing
The jingling is unheard
        Once so familiar
        So familiar I now often tremble

Who says this:
That doesn't mean anything?

No, that doesn't mean anything either if—
If you part the morning rain
And find me, hooded in a blue raincoat,
And like the people waiting for the bus by the roadside
Standing still in your absorbed gaze.

LOOKING OUT

Sounds intertwine with sounds;
A clamor shakes this morning lightly.
Pull up the window blind
And let the street scene in to be near us.
Standing abreast on the road are the sun and the tree shadows.
Buildings and buildings, listless like us,
Look toward the distances,
And the blue sky
Is seldom or never like a sky;
As the fabulous heart of warmth
That always brightens the look of silence.

We are always surprised, therefore, surprised to find
The coincidental gathering would turn out to be
An intentional arrangement.

If one has to see the empty vastness of winds and rains
Before he can remember the appearance of the cosmos,
    Its many aspects
    Forming and disappearing, disappearing and forming—
If my wisdom is an arm long enough
    To reach that unknowable blank.
I will certainly be able to feel anxiety crouching
Just as one can feel the heart throbbing against his flesh.

GROPING

With dexterity I raise my hand
To knock for the silence to open
Imagining that, upon striking this solid door
One would hear a positive sound.
Who from the outer region is pushing on the revolving door
While already the white border has turned toward someone else?
Evening and autumn always hesitate—
True, we always like to wait unknowingly
For the corn to be laden with ears, for meanings
And then speculate
that all fruit will be ripe in this fashion—
And, like the seeds waiting to be sown,
Cherish all sorts of expectations
Silently gazing at the black door moving toward us.

MALTREATMENT

The entire street of the wireless
Treads on its own tail.
O Maltreatment!
The long nylon leg is nailed on
Velvet as black as eternity.

Often, unlike a customer I stand
Before familiar windows
To mirror my own shadow
My strange and alien shadow
Which is piled among the confused hustle
    Of pedestrians, time, cars, and sounds
I am happy, horrifyingly happy, waiting to be sold
Like the goods reflected on this glass from the windows of another shop.

Often I like to mirror myself in this way, being
Wholly delighted to
Use my own paleness reflected from gaudiness
To maltreat myself.

Huang Yung

THE FEEL OF MELANCHOLY

Unable to distinguish all these:
Laid on the jointed iron sheets are
A heap of nails
And some toothed junks.
I think I am arranging for a massacre—
Just like having all the snakes in one den.

But these are solid and all of a piece,
Piling themselves up, piling;
And afloat . . . But
They are no vessels
Nor is there any sound.

VARIATION*

I

These are some roots
Entwined and all-pervading
In the dark of my body

I am inert
Easily rotten
In this summer in this summer
I plant with my own hands some poison ivy
An ivy so endearing

II

If I rage
If in the dazzling sunlight I look
        hard at a fresh-cropped girl
If I hurry among crowds

*This translation is a revision from two versions done by the author himself and by
Mr. Louis Tsen.

I am only a heap of boring trifles
    some causeless trembling
I dissect myself so unpleasantly
And restring these fragments for others
Equally unpleasant

III

You are only a number of tooth-marked ruts
You are only a number of crisscrossing streets
    that lead nowhere
In windless afternoons
I always hold your pulse like a handful of cooling noises

IV

It is in your conceited generosity
It is in your low-priced superiority
It is in your luxuriant ignorance
I plant with my own hands some poison ivy, ah
An ivy so endearing

DIRGE

This is the only rose in the city
Rising like a flame in the bustling blank
The gray river that glitters in the pupils of the blind
    Flows unawares bearing the shadows of towering buildings
On the newly-painted iron benches some of the aged are sunning themselves
And the sauntering on the plaza is carefree
In a slackening yawn, there it seems
Something is speeding

For example, in the steam-heated days we say:
When pretty bodies cover the beach
There we have the summer

Huang Yung

And, from a faraway street comes
Like a desperate cry
The screech of the brakes

On the west side of the city, on the west side
Crowds are stalled and stalled, waiting without protest
For the rumbling of subway trains
To roll over their covetousness
I, too, howl and rush like a wild wheel
I, too, pass through the shadows of many buildings obscuring the sky
As through a forest of crosses
O a forest of crosses
Where, where the heaped corpses of the city are laid

What follows is blank
A boundless blank like
The snow waiting to be trampled, such deep-cut footprints!
Then after a while, a long long while
The nothingness of centuries passes by
And suddenly all the flowers of civilization turn into ashes
The wind batters lanes and streets of decayed leaves
In my cold cold eyes—ah!
The city dies once again
And I am in for a premature death
And my desire, on the west side of the city
Now, too, lies in the exposed ruins
And crouches there humble and bare
Waiting for violation

And on the east side of the city
Girls sway weakly, they are
    Clothes to be dried on the lines
    Or lines on which to dry clothes
Children are wide-spreading ringworms
Laborers are rusted chassis
Scattered between rubbish heaps and factories
And my all-quiet walls on the east side of the city
Are founded on the simmering of desire

O days confined within walls
    days of peddling one's heart
    days when solitudes clash with solitudes
    The waves and surges of past days now
Scour:
Now the remnant of spring
Is unused shreds of paper flying about the streets
Is a cup of leftover wine
But whose round shoulder is it
But who drives me now to run toward yesterday
                    more yesterdays?

O master of the overbearing
I am familiar with your voice
You are the hubbub that ceaselessly splits the ear
Your breath comes from epidemic diseases
Your gesture is the recurring thump of the piston
You strike me like a spark leaping up from an anvil

I *am* the loneliness that splashes with desire
    Forgive me then
I am settled and used to the peace of being ruled
Because I am familiar with this kind of positiveness

So the only rose
Is extinguished
Through its still petals
I can see the neurotic trembling of the past
Through the cracked windshield
In the pitchy background of clusters of wound-scars
Balanced and stable
The corpse of this city
Looms like a plate
O still
Still holding much the look of some girls
    And inches of soot
    And inches of car dust

李

红

CHI HUNG (CH'I TOA-P'ANG), 1927–.

b.   Honan Province.

Lieutenant colonel in the Chinese Navy.

Statement:

I need peace. I need the "True I" that can hold me in the midst of all other forces, the "True I" that can make me stay away from the fashionable modes of the times even when the forces are strong. I write not out of a sense of responsibility but purely for the supreme delight of the heart. If one day I should publish them in book form, it will be for those who can feel and enjoy the same interest as I do.

——from a letter to Ya Hsien

What I mean by "giving-forth" in terms of directness and exactness is reproducing through objects and events the complete form received by the heart. It is not intuition, not description, but the insulated, uncovered and unostentatious form itself as it has been received by the heart.

——from "Aspects of Poetry"

LIGHT ON THE SURFACE OF THE SEA

Like a good-looking girl,
The surface of the sea bends down to look into
The windowpanes of my cabin,
                              smiling
And exposing her snow-white teeth.

A pure girl's clean soul
In which pliant feelings grow slowly
Cream-colored, such elegance.

Right before our eyes comes the flashing sun,
Like bushes and bushes of silver,
      Like a girl's brooch.
It will become a bride.
And all these come to complete her beauty.
Therefore, people think of her;
And for the same reason, they become irritated.

THE FUSION OF SENSES

Winter days.
Flux of wind in small steps across the room.
Landscapes on the wall: exquisitely printed
Appearance of Taipei
Still buoyant with spring's feel,

Calls up warmth—
The sun now seen now unseen
The moon
And the chafing pan
                  for warming our feet of last year

And the linen handsomely dyed and woven
Love

And luminously smooth bodies breathing orchid-smell
Her shadow

And memory
And wine
    which we drink in the Chinese new year and wedding parties
And paper flowers and lamps

The frost is covering
    The twigs stripped of fruit
    The grass turning yellow by the riverside
A distant thought, an expectation

Calls up warmth—
A sounding horn and a song,
Confidence and flag.

MALE WORKERS BACK FROM NIGHT DUTIES

So drooping
These plum trees, so pale.
Night is a more relentless killing.
Coming back from a lost battle with this kind of enemies
In this kind of disagreeable morning, making us
See such decaying wax-yellow petals
And
Wet-cold pistils.

No girls will be so kind as to
Put them to their red red lips.

Nothing will be fit for them except
This cold-white
Mist-fouling morning and
The life
Of their women.

THE WHITE AMBULANCE

Virgin boys
        and
Virgin girls
Dressed in white clothes hold each other's hands.
On the most rugged road
The red cross flickers
              a pale light.
(Heavenly kingdom.)
            Thus they wait
Beneath the sickened white cover.
Angels sing
        spreading their white lower arms
        and
Hands as clean as the moon on the fence.
Dressed in white, holding wine upon their palms
Virgin boys
        and
Virgin girls

        Beneath the sad white cover
        At the call of the red-cross light

Angels sing
With such great grief.

MORNING

Toward the church a lady's green hat
At whose brim a sunflower
Which smells of a peaceful heart and the accessible worship
Is flowing
With refreshing air
I think of that silent lady
Who can fully express herself in a smile.
She is my fiancée

REEDS

We will not narrate in this fashion.
In a whole day's temptation our lips
Should be closed in order to preserve a fullness
So that we will be able to prevent
Those exhausted people
Those people toiling abroad
From becoming uneasier.

Even if—
    Amidst all reflections
    Amidst loneliness and the light of death—
They remember you
They see you.

AN EGRET

    An egret
    Lingering here before he returns
    After the sun has set
    In the obscure emptiness
        In the deep
            A call.

    As some sort of will
    Within an uneasy, indistinct
        memory

    (a kind of weariness).

SIGNAL LAMPS ON THE RAILWAY CROSSROADS

Potters cannot
Artisans cannot
The girls' smile and even their dreams
Cannot make

These flowers
   That do not belong to this city.
   Short short in stature
   These purple-colored
   Loneliness-spreading
   Faces.

SONS AND DAUGHTERS

 The arrangement of disquietude.
 Battlements and battlements
 Dahlias and pine trees
 The thriving of dreams
 Ailments of hope.
 There was never a more vivid dream
 Urgent and pain-giving
 Without hope
 Soaring too high, higher than

 They
 —(Their sleep sweet and
     true)

 The arrangement of sadness
 and
   takeover.

Chi Hung

FERRY

We walk past the flower forum
              Girls
Walk past the chrysanthemum and marigold garden.
In a season like this
The chrysanthemum sticks out its body and there
The marigold leans.

We walk past the rose bushes
                    Girls
Facing the morning sun while the red roses are blooming
Attractively like you.

The white roses' buds in
The sobriety of dawning
Are cleaner and more beautiful. Girls,
They can fill the flower baskets of your breasts.

And we walk past.
We have to go to the lattices that have a shivering sound
And to grey guns and to the
Cold, cold steel cables.
We will see again, (not knowing where),
        Girls.

CHOU MENG-TIEH, 1920–.

b.   Honan Province.

"I was born on December 30, 1920, in Che-ch'uan, Honan Province. I had been a soldier, grade and high school teacher, shopkeeper and librarian. Now I am maintaining my existence by selling secondhand books on a street stall."

Poetry: *The Realm of Solitude* (1959)
        Huan-hun-ts'ao (*"Soul-returning" Grass,* 1965)

Statement:

Sea: wide for fishes to frisk/Sky: open for bird to fly. No poet can be without this vastness of mind. *If I did not go into Hell, who else would?* No poet can be without this readiness. *Girdle becomes loose: no regret,/to become haggard for her.* No poet can be without this determination. *How charming the green mountains appear to me!/I appear the same to the green mountains, I believe.* No poet can be without this intimate subtlety.

JUNE

Poem I

Reclining on what is not mine, I hear myself
What is obscurely beyond myself
And yet obviously inside myself
The surge of June.

Cold from where has never been cold,
The millennial riverbed shivers,
Issuing from an over-stout yawning,
Scattering a bitter smile like a snow-tear
On a black and thin rose thorn.

The first night when frost fell, the grapes and the vine
Mumbled their dreams beneath the stars—
They met always like strangers,
Dreaming the plum blooming over the fields,
The dead trees singing-dancing round a fire;
Dreaming the Heavenly Kingdom in the shape of a little hempen bag
And Jesus not the last willing cobbler.

JUNE

Poem II

In June on the fields after harvest
When everything becomes lean
There, beyond the sunset, a wooden bell chimes alone
Driving up a flight of silences—white feathers, white claws
Circling above the spire: Praises, responses . . .

This is the fiercest season of snakes and apples
The sun floats up every night from the Black Sea

Epicurus gulped down the bitter artemisia wine
And buried under the pillow of pure rationalization
A petal of camellia

Pupils behind the eyelids decide to look only into themselves
And never to comment whose heart has seven holes!
When the calamus turns green, some weeping will flow day and night—
Why seek for divination from my hand (itself cracked) holding the
    tortoise shell?
In the depth of smoke and water, who remains awake tonight in the
    roaring water?
Gorgeous as a snake rod, the cry from the above
Corresponds to the bell—That is a star
An eye Moses hung in the sky!
How many bleeding feet are at rest in the midst of groaning
The earth sparkles with tears. In one night crows' heads turn white!

AT THE END OF THE WATERCOURSE

At the end of the watercourse
There is no end, there is no water,
But a stretch of floating scent
Cold in the eyes, in the ears and on the clothes.

You are the fountainhead;
I am ripples in the fountain.
We met
    in the beginning of the cold, the end of the cold
Like the winds and the eyes of the winds

Waking up suddenly, transported to look into each other,
To see you in me, me in you,
To see you above, behind, before and around:
But a smile, and a thousand years gone forever!
You have a flower to bloom in your heart,
Blooming before the first petal swells.

Who is the first petal?
The first cold? the unfading ripples?

At the end of the watercourse
There is no end, there is no water,
But a stretch of floating scent
Cold in the eyes, in the ears and on the clothes.

EMBRACE OF EMPTINESS

Embrace the drifting—the black snow,
The unseizable frigidity and beauty
From your eyes
And the silence threatening to burst out from your sockets.

One can almost hear every thread of hair
Whisper sibilantly—
Such horrifying distance.
My seventh finger clamors furiously
That you are an empty-fruit
And I the fire-core that is not yet reduced to ashes.

On Thanksgiving Day, where you go
(Dust-free are your shoes)
The ringing of springs, the fragrance of flowers like snow
Will close around you—and kiss your soles
The blood-dripping past.

Coming from you and returning to you
A day of sunset
Suddenly glows and suddenly dims
Toward every inch of emptiness.
Where is the home of the frightened wild geese?
East of emptiness, speechless. West of emptiness, speechless.
South of emptiness, speechless. North of emptiness, speechless.

Chou Meng-tieh

REFLECTIONS—RIDING ON A BUS

How I wish I were blindly rocking, drifting
Toward the distance, toward the farther end
Like a drunken boat
—Never to stop!

Evening colors fill the windows. Such hurrying joy!
Scenery retreats successively behind us
In a fashion, tired but leisurely elegant
     One uproar of applause
     After another swelling from
     One bowing to the audience before the curtain

After we have passed the Bridge of the Eight Immortals
We think of the goddesses among the clouds
Whom the empyrean cold never seems to bother
How could they take off the worldly dust
Just like taking off last night's fading rouge?
     The same blood and flesh
     The same flame reaching a thousand feet high
     Coiled on the hair, a thousand feet long

For whom is the flute blown? For whom does a flower turn red?
West of the Milky Way, east of the Milky Way
They say, between two hearts, among footprints
There is always a connecting red silken thread*—
     But where is the witness? When Time is like a high wind
     Carrying perilous waves and a dark moon, today's cloud
     Is no longer yesterday's rose. . . .

Next stop will be the Golden Bird Garden
How come my heart beats so strangely!
My eyes burnt for seeing the mountains
How come when they now appear in dripping green
I feel so grievous as if I were walking into snow and mist!

*A red silken thread often suggests matrimonial relation.

I remember last year when I came here
The bright pomegranate flowers scorched our sight
And now the tree is heavily laden

ONE NIGHT IN THE MOUNTAINS

Wrapped up by darkness just like
A pearl wrapped up by shells—
My soul matures,
Growing into a circle, into a glittering drop.

You only have to flip your fingers
And darkness will scatter down in pieces;
There will be starlight, valleys of cloud-dream, forests of leaf-words
All gurgling out from a pointing finger.

And I have been there—
An instantaneous truth!—there among rocks, upon waters
Among flowers, beneath the grass—there and everywhere!

Awakened from a thousand years. Roaring winds from shoreless shores and
Wolves' howl rising and falling like dashing waves
Blast at me—Ah! my alarm clock.

THE PASSER-THROUGH-THE-WALLS

Scorching and yet chilling,
Your traces are winds—
All the walls, though cast in bronze,
Prick up their ears,
And as if attracted by curses
They move in great multitudes toward you.

Every corner of darkness is pasted with your eyes.
Your eyes are nets,
Netting directions—directions toward you
And directions leading away from you.

The Hunter lights up your window every night.
Your window, sometimes widely open,
Sometimes closed tightly;
Sometimes it is darker when it is open than closed.
Your eyes are filled with fluorescence, with yellow dust-mist . . . .

The Hunter says that only he has your key.
The Hunter says if you happen to leave the window open
He will gently close it for you . . . .

YÜ KUANG-CHUNG, 1928–.

b.   Fukien Province.

Associate professor of English at Taiwan Normal University; co-founder of the *Blue Stars Poetry Society* and editor of its publications.

Poetry: *Stalactite* (1960)
　　　　Hollowe'en (1960)
　　　　Associations of the Lotus (1964)
　　　　A Youth from Wu-ling (1967)

The author considers his two earlier volumes not worthy of mentioning.

Statement:

Naturally we also hope for sympathy from more readers, but we never place popularization over art. Naturally we have emotions to express, but we do not wish people to take writing poetry or reading poetry as a form of emotional release. We are against romanticism, but we also disdain to ask aid from classicism, for in the representations of emotions and interpretations of the rational, we prefer the digging of the subconscious, the cold observation of the intellect, and the high awareness of our own existence. We are willing to understand science, but we demand the transcending of mechanism; we want to break through the narrow concept of traditional aesthetics and to consider abstract beauty as the purest beauty, and the illogical as the logic of beauty.

　　　　—— from "The Many-prickled Cactus of the Cultural Desert"

Yü Kuang-chung

HOU I SHOOTING NINE SUNS [1]

Straddling upon Taishan's highest peak, overlooking the cracked vast plains,
Behind me, the boiling Yellow Sea cooking a cauldron of serpents and whales,
I pull my Crow-Bow and put on piercing arrows from Ch'i,
And stare at the nine suns with eyes of autumn vultures.

Phoenixes, now ashes; the Ch'i-lin [2] thirsted to death; comets appear in
    daytime.
Black-burnt jungles stretch out billions of convulsed palms of devils.
I rage; I hate and disdain the tyrannical suns.
Rage endows me with the Killer's mettle. A human,
I dare nine gods to duel with me, wanting
To shoot down one-tenth of the cosmos with one arrow,
Fearing not nemesis, fearing not life imprisonment in flames!

I trust my heroic will to the expeditionary arrow,
Which lays in ambush in my bosom, a marathon racer with rays;
I trust my warrior's determination to the unbending bow,
Which struggles with full strength to straighten my fate's string;
I kindle my staring eyeballs with a rebel's rage.
The nine suns roar, rolling like hedgehogs of light, piercing me with
                incandescent javelings;
With booming laughters, they flout that I will be blinded like bats.

A sudden release of the fingers, quick rebouncing of the string, the arrow
    speeds upward.
Nine thousand million miles' distance gives in to its speed.
Then, convulsion of the cosmos, breaking of Heavenly River's banks, panic
    from times untold.

---

[1] The myth has it that in the time of Emperor Yao (2357?–2255?) there were ten
suns which scorched the ground, burnt up every form of vegetation, causing much
disorder and many deaths upon earth. Since each sun was bound up on a large crow,
Hou I, the archer, with a will to deliver the earth from the disaster, shot down nine
of the suns, leaving one to give the earth light and warmth.

[2] The ch'i-lin is a fabulous, auspicious animal. Its appearance is often associated with
the birth of a great sage.

The fall of a god, the destruction of a star, the meteorites splashing on the
      ground like a red waterfall!
Nü Wo,[3] refine more rocks to repair the firmament!
Behind Yen-tzu Mountain are now buried nine suns' corpses.
Now, the arrow holder is empty, the vast space is empty.
Now, a million torches are held up in the west to celebrate the burial of the
      gods.

But this is not evening. I turn toward the disturbing sea
And spread out my arms and shout to the rising tenth sun:
"Lone God, I leave you in the dark sky to shine this world.
I am gods' rebel, I am the sun-shooter, I am Hou I!"

ANSWER?

Always want to raise a pithecanthrope's shrill cry
To stab to death the solitude oppressing me

Unable to stand forever on the equator
In the noontide of the autumnal equinox
Tread away my own shadows
Therefore, my melancholy
Gains length

Sleep-walking in the dreariness composed of clamors
I often get lost among steel designs
O so wide, the century; freezing cold, the time
I had stood upon the banks of Lake Michigan
Looking across it, at mirages of Chicago

O so wide, the century; freezing cold, the time
Ch'angan in the Han Dynasty; men in Wu-ling[1]

---

[3] See note 1 in Ya Hsien's "On Streets of China."

[1] Wu-ling, the five imperial sepulchres of the Han Dynasty, became later an area
where poets, heroes, and worthies were active.

The green light is off. Police sirens and trumpets take the place
Of drums in history and the accompaniment of tears. How come
I am constantly blocked by red lights' angry eyes? How come
I am constantly misplaced on time and space's graph?
How come I am constantly stranded here?

And once after four, all the shadows of buildings
Climb toward me; once after four
Rootless fear breaks out
On the nerve's net pass crisscrossly
Many high-speed feelings, towards no man's land

And men always in Wu-ling
Ch'angan always in the Han Dynasty

Always, after four
The world takes down its mask
Always, after four
I no longer recognize the 20th century
I no longer recognize myself
(And all memory is carved on
The other side of the tombstone)
I want to throw down the mirror, I want to run out amuck

But night is always so kind
Pure velvet black
Is my protective color. Let me take time to
Ask, from the secret codes of the constellations
For an answer to abstract beauty

UPON THE MANY-HUMPED CAMELS

Riding thus upon a horde of many-humped camels
We return to China, toward southwest west
Huge black-winged gulls following the white runway at the stern
Constantly pretend to take off but never really do

We divine from the ancient bronze sun
And see by which side the profile of our tutelary god falls
Seven thirty. (Seven thirty? What significance does time have
Upon this blue Gobi, except to date mermaids?)
We use this copper coin to bribe the night
To buy us some broken dreams slanting to 40°
Or insomnia, to listen to the aquatic rhapsody
Cables perform beneath five thousand feet
Sometimes, we find even this is too expensive
Then, night finds us a handful of falling stars

Upon the Alaskan sea, all that have a nose caught a cold
All the fish caught a cold. We hear
The cachalots sneezing continuously in the distances
When the wind blows on our face, all the waves will be sneezing

We are at great leisure, leaning upon the port to sun ourselves
And wonder if the sea calves will feel the same way
We are busy, always swinging like a pendulum
Back and forth between graves and toys
Old affairs of the New Continent—new generation of our Old Country
Between Vancouver and the Orient, we swing
Between the T'ang Dynasty and Hollywood, we swing
Seasick pills are dueling with vomiting inside the stomach
We are busy

In the passage beyond the Aleutian Islands, whales have a cold
We have a cold. How we wish we could
Sneeze ten feet tall, like them!

Seagulls chase us, through the foggy season of Canada
We are homing travellers from the Streets of the T'ang People [1]
Thus, dreaming upon the many-humped camels

[1] Because of the unrivaled prosperity, both culturally and economically, of the T'ang Dynasty, the Chinese people have been referred to with reverence, as the T'ang people. Thus, Chinatowns in all foreign countries have been called *t'ang-jen-chieh*, i.e., Streets of the T'ang People.

We return to China, toward southwest west
On the Streets of the T'ang People, there are no T'ang people, no princes
No tributary caravans of camels, no high priests from India
No law-breaking Li Po
(Fortunately enough, no potbellied An Lu-shan to knock us down)[2]
We dare not ask the way from the yellow people in the Chop Suey
    restaurants
Dare not ask them which direction is the Yen-ch'iu Gate
(That day we must have lost our way
Although we came from a country of compasses)

Between blue and blue, we draw curves
Toward southwest, following the slide of latitudes
Between icecaps and icecaps, who, minute as he is,
Is playing bowling?

Seeing the typhoon instigate all the waves to mutiny
We practise ropewalking upon parabolas and vomit
Drawing out all the scholarship of a Ph.D. in Hydraulics
We eat fruits and swear that we will never leave fruit-growing
    places anymore
(It must be good to be a Newton, not inventing anything! We think)
The sea holds both the left and the right sides and look in from
    the round windows to see who,
Bursting into heroic laughters, throws out tons and tons of toys

On the semi-tropical sea, stars are pedantic
Familiar clouds pile upon one another at the horizon
The bow ploughs up many flying fish
When we review the Ryukyu Islands

In this way, we return to the Eastern Hemisphere, not quite excited yet
Although we are recovering from our nostalgia

---

[2] An Lu-shan, originally from one of the barbaric tribes, held a prominent position in the palace in the T'ang Dynasty when Emperor Hsüan-tsung debauched his country in his indulgence in a surpassing beauty Yang Kuei-fei, who, presumably, had later adopted An as son. An rose in rebellion in 755 and was killed by his adopted sons.

Although on the cherry-blossom islands we had been nailed
With the hairpins of Madame Butterfly
In this way, our whims flow, upon the many-humped camels
Returning to China, yes, we finally return to
Such a China—no Loyang, no Ch'angan ³
No tall Hsüan-wu Gate to dwarf the envoys from the Barbaric West
No odorous knees to rub flat the stone steps of the Tai-ming Palace
Calling three times, "Long Live the Heavenly Khan!"

Riding thus upon the humps, we return, as the Sirius rises
Our eyes do not indulge in mirages anymore
The *Encyclopedia of Waters* is in the knapsack; thirst is beneath the tongue
Tears are also salty, no way to relieve our tribulation
And we are travellers from the distant Streets of the T'ang People
Although we do not see any people from the T'ang Dynasty
We ruminate and ruminate, upon the humps
Using the last setting sun left to us by Hou I ⁴
To divine the victory and loss in Cholu.⁵

TURFAN ¹

At last the irresistible fatigue comes to attack
The all-black cat of nonbeing squatting on our face
Let the red mercury ebb in the haemal system
To experience the dead silence after the inundation
Thus stranded on this plane of death
We die for love and line abreast our corpses

Night is cubic—although time, like a rat, is gnawing
Stars on sentry above the roof pass commands
While we make moistness under it
And make all that swell swell
As the warm Simmons bed is turfaning us

³ Loyang and Ch'angan had been capitals in many brilliant dynasties.
⁴ See "Hou I Shooting Nine Suns" by the same author, p. 119.
⁵ The battlefield where the ancient war between Huangti and Tz'u-yu took place, during which the latter was defeated. See Ya Hsien's "On Streets of China."

With a restless hand-gesture
We throw away the art of Lei-chu,[2] and put on savagery
The primitive epidemic forest bewilders us
As we exchange warmth and rub flintstones
Attempting to uproot all life
Attempting to poison the counter-mate, then poison ourselves

Blood, the liquid given to boiling most easily
Is already kindled in each other's alcohol lamp
And we fan the roar of the Red Sea
Even if you closed your Venetian blinds I could still smell
The scorching of desire, white smoke leaking out
From all wide pores of the sweat glands

At least we can forget the moistness on the ground
And with your moistness prove yourself a female animal
At least we can forget the slicing of limbs by maggots
And with incandescent heat brand the marks of occupation
Forget the stiff cold and the black eyesight of an empty socket
Living—in an absolutely dependable *now*
Forget one body within another

When vertebrates use the sun on the planet's other side
Or the man-made moonlight inside a building
When they push the grindstone on the watch face
And take narcotics on different wheels
Looking out from different zippers
To ride on picnicking clouds with eyes

[1] The Turfan were one of the many barbaric tribes in ancient China known for their savagery.

[2] Lei-chu, Huangti's (2698 B.C.) queen, who first discovered the use of silk.

Yü Kuang-chung

SIT DOWN TO SEE CLOUDS RISE

Walk to the source of the stream
And sit down to see clouds rise
—Wang Wei (701–761)

When I sit down to see clouds rise, sun-clouds glare at me
With white eyes, green eyes. So I think of the remote Juan Chi,[1]
Of him at the end of the third century,
Weeping bitterly like me, like me sitting under
The Lovesick Tree that knows not what the South is

To see clouds rise,
To see clouds rise—the fickle space throwing white and green eyes—
To see if what *whites* me today had ever *greened* me with sunshine—
To see clouds rise—who throws white and green eyes?
I never wept, never wept like our Wei poet.[2]
I happen to walk to the source of the stream: no road to go,
So I sit down to see clouds rise and try to tell the directions of winds.

When clouds rise, everything changes. The universe looks on,
Watching the whims of sun-clouds take form, come and go,
How from nothing comes something, how it escapes easily
When I close my eyes to see incoming birds
Swim into the breast-cleaning layers of clouds
When the dream smashes itself on the glass-top of my watch

from the T'aishan.[3]

[1] Juan Chi (210–263).

[2] Juan Chi.

[3] From a Tu Fu (712–770) poem, the last four lines of which may be translated as follows:

> "Rolling chest: in it are born layers of clouds,
> Eyelids strained to open by incoming birds from afar.
> Ah! to stand atop the highest peak
> To see: how tiny the rest of the hills!"
> — Looking at the T'aishan

HYPERBOREAN TREPIDATION

Such paleness, the season! I do not know whether
Spring will have a prenatal death.
Why all the windows of my little study are northward?
Why every night, when a sick cat mews in the strong wind,
My murals brighten sombrely
In the will-o'-the-wisp of the Ursa Minor?
The Pole Star is the patriarch of the Eskimos,
Aged like the universe. All night I listen
To the Eskimos, with their whale-bone knives, crisply knock down
Many many icicles from his white beards
All night I think—

Next spring I should build for myself
A greenhouse with all four sides facing south
So that, waking up from the luxury of Sunday,
I can listen to the sun calling, above the roof,
Calling out to sunflowers: Eyes right! Eyes left!
And outside the long broad bay windows,
Colors contend in roaring chatters. Partridges from distances
Murmur with a French trumpet
To hypnotize the sexy clouds.

DOUBLE BED

Let war go on beyond the double bed.
Lying upon your long, long slope,
We listen to stray bullets, like roaring fireflies,
Whiz over your head, my head,
Whiz over my moustache and your hair.
Let coups d'état, revolutions howl around us;
At least love is on our side.
At least before daybreak, we will be safe.
When everything is no longer reliable,

Yü Kuang-chung

I lie on your elastic slope.
Tonight, even if there were landslides and earthquakes,
The worst would be but to fall into your low, low basin.
Let them raise flags, blow horns over the highland,
At least there are six feet of rhythm that are ours.
At least before sunrise, you will be all mine,
Still slippery, still soft, still hot enough to cook,
A kind of pure, fine madness.
Let night and death at the border of darkness
Start an everlasting siege the thousandth time.
Only we descend abruptly along the spiral line: Heavenly Kingdom is below;
And get caught into the beautiful whirlpool of your four limbs.

CHANG MO (CHANG TEH-CHUNG), 1932–.

b.   Anhui Province.

Serves in the Chinese Navy; executive editor of the *Epoch Poetry Quarterly* (with Ya Hsien and Lo Fu).

Poetry: *The Edge of Purple* (1964)

Statement:
There is no fixed form, language, or technique that can yoke modern poetry. The perspective of modern poetry is built upon its vast and endless change. It always begins, it always builds, forever expanding within itself all new expressions and new sensibilities that are inaccessible in life. The modern poet is never content, never really solitary and never ceases to function.

FOURTEENERS

1

Let the sinking earth become still and disappear.
Clouds of your thought bring us
Through passes and passes of your solemn heart
And call:
To escape into the long sky, long sky with streams of glittering light—
Glitter, perhaps, beautiful with
Shreds trailing.
Proud like a pillar, that fountain.

Let your short hair fly and flutter
In Time, frisk and go after
Those meditative lovers,
Those meditative lovers.
Letter brimming with blazing words.
Life spreads before us.   Children in March.

2

Like rain, veins of the eucalyptus clamber up my window.
Winds blow them up. The tree longs for growth:
Slender fingers, crisp, green hair and
Dense feelings; it calls so as
To fasten clusters of flowers of clouds.

Say it is love; love's song needs no sign.
Set it between lips.
Hide it in the auditory canal.
Let it rock and rock.
Say it is love; love is the wind of a meditative man.

Drift, piano of flowing water. A girl from the North,
She comes very near and goes like mist.
Even if we never meet again, like rain,
The eucalyptus still stands strong in our hearts.

3

We often spend time with solitude: musing is the truest wealth.
Through evening gardens, sun's shade is already far away.
The earth has long forgotten robust singing.
All things become still: mystery wakes in birth.

What friendship! all over distant coasts not yet traveled,
Where oysters grow with strangers' steps.
I distinctly remember everything is in rhythm
And shores, water's surface, tropical fishes and permanent trees
Still emotionally embrace our interior.

So let them spread out in their own fashion.
I know how to harken, praise and correspond.
Night descends: stars floating with creamy light.
This moment: only memory,
Only looking into, only Time and its every . . . .

EDGE OF PURPLE

A shadow undulates among the hundred flowers
Harkening to the reviving reading and singing that fall
On clean tips of branches along brimming fragrance of
The water of spring
The water of spring
Bushes of dark hair, fleecy tufts of early grass
A mirror-lake, an orchid sombre—
Purple-lovers, they say, are blessed
Purple-lovers, mutated they say,
To gird up a dress at the waist with unseizable colors
And heart—how deep is the half we caress and caress!

Didn't we once enter the low-breathing
Dream-sea? Didn't we meet when you

Lightly shook your wave-hurrying flower-umbrella
As if turning yourself over again and again
Breaking into sounds . . . ?
What is the rhythm that runs against you?
No reason to climb upward,
　　　　　　no reason to drink up the all-wet interior
Like the fog's sound and light
　　　　　　glueing up the white edges of our lips
And with silence smash our flesh?

The sun reflects, the sun releases, the sun reveals
The plough and the diversified timbre
Sow seeds on her purple
Plaited curls. Oh—How could one say that this is a lie?
If it is not the rainbow erected by nature toward the evening
If you would not mind our overly-heavy steps
Why don't you lift your skirt just slightly
To throw out a handful of stars
　　　　　　　　and jump upon them.

I STAND IN THE WIND

I stand in the wind, drinking with flying sands and stones;
Dance feverishly with my slender limbs
And sing the Big Wind Song, pouring out my heart's knot
For the first time: I have never been so joyful.

Thoughts fall onto howling waves.
Full eye's reach of water: so blurred, Creation.
I want to come close to it, with full life's force,
To fly over,
To swim across,
And lick the salt made by the hot-tempered sea.
My heart's dense forests, its moist nights and
Querulous stars suddenly metamorphose into many frisking dragons.

I stand in the wind,
All my veins like darting arrows,
Flights after flights,
Blood sprinkled on the waste, unloosened, unsoftened earth.

>   Flowers leap for joy.
>   Birds make music.
>   Cedars sing the song of growth.

I burn and dance—
This season of big winds in celebration,
Nature's concerto,
Resonant among my heart's branches.
O what makes it so
Profound, limpid, so cold and
So distant and enigmatic?

So distant and enigmatic!
But I am a huge tree of a thousand leaves
Stretching immense strong arms
Abundantly upward—
In the wind, in the merging wind,
My robust drinking is also a child's natural expression.

HSIUNG HUNG (HU MEI-TZU), 1940–.

b.   Taiwan Province.

She is an artist-designer.

Poetry: *The Golden Pupa* (1968)

No statement.

BURNING UNDER THE SEA

Blue roars in.
Many precious visions, sadly
Withdraw—
"Under the sea will be burning
    At the edge of corals corals stand
    At the edge of the edge of corals more corals stand
"And your name is undying brightness
You said:
"Lift your face and look at me—

"Don't drink alone the dripping sadness of the story.
The rainy season is over. Do not refuse the golden sunlight anymore
Do not continue to design your tomb, a pile of
Three thousand six hundred crystal layers
Situated between the closing and opening of eyes in the lengthless dream

"Lift your face and look at me—

"The rainy season is over. Convalescence
Lies behind the gray veil of exhaustion, waiting to perform
With the elegant movements of a ballet dancer
                    waiting for you, waiting for you"

And visions sadly withdraw
From the chill soil; a sun-loving little plant
Timidly lifts its head, looking at you—

ASSOCIATIONS IN BLACK

Dusk is eyes after crying
Looking at me, with a full flame of emotion.

But at length the visible
And the invisible—

The five-thousand-colored fires all die out,
    (You cannot stand my belief).
All darkened, the boulevards; all darkened, the wide long bridges.
The Satan-hand that conducts fate is arranging
    (The long hand chases the short hand, ready to overtake it any time)
Arranging—
The darker death in a dark night at quarter past seven.

I startle and learn: the black hour is over;
Nothing can ever revive and
You don't have to face to the west—despairingly.

THE WHITE BIRD IS PRIMEVAL

And the unebbing thought nears
The island, rising from the environs of your statue.
And distance is an arm too long
Casting a net which catches 1957,
Our first acquaintance.

The endless white is ripening perfection
Enriching life. In the Southern morning
A low tuft of grass at our feet trembles
    (As many other low tufts of grass did)
At its direction not yet determined
It is why, god, I choose you
    In a Southern morning.

Eternity must necessarily exist
In this extreme white
And the engraving knife says:
    Remember with your firm standing stature
    That which holds my soft heart—

I AM ALREADY GOING TOWARD YOU

You stand beneath the floral lamps on the opposite bank.
All chords are muted. I want to wade across this circular pond,
Wade across this blue glass inscribed with water lilies.
I am the only soprano.

The only. I am a carving hand
                    carving sempiternal sadness
Which lives in a smile, sempiternal sadness.
All chords are muted. The globe turns only eastward.
I beg, on this smooth paper-leaf of permanence,
Beg for the convergence of today and tomorrow.

But the lamp-mist does not move. I go toward you.
I am already going toward you.
All chords are muted
I am the only soprano.

UNTITLED

Coming out from expectancy,
Please ascend this step, treading upon tinkling notes.
There are colors coming in pomp;
There are rivers and seas coming in a high roar.
My god, please ascend this step.
The luxury of loneliness after you . . .

Lead me to rise up; looking back is the distant earth.
Say, believe that we exist together or die together
And wait for me waiting at this long step
The background is timelessness.
My god, please lead me to rise up

Coming out from the far far tract of sight
Oh! Blue, please ascend my step.
The bustle of voices after you . . . .

DEMANDING A PROFILE

From the twenty-six-colored road of happiness leading
To another kingdom of music,
Our song is a white rose with head uplifted
Fed in the vase by the water of a gold morning cloud.

Forgive me for my yesterday for the evil fowl of yesterday's nightmare
Fearfully pecks at me
Waking up only to find my pain in pieces
Scattered over the ground: In May that year
Someone demanded of a stranger his profile
Because he looked like you.

Pluck a bud of song from the other end of the road of happiness
Forgive yesterdays and remember the very first day,
The very first day in a long long summer
The window of your studio opened toward the south.

A WORLD IN WHITE

Let me put you in a landscape.
The streets are like girdles, white girdles
Stretching far into the smoke, far into a dream that has no footfalls.

Twenty miles, twenty thousand miles or beyond
We can walk to the end tirelessly.
The shore and end of the road are icicles where summer is frozen

—Do you love the sea, the sea that shines with white scales?
You are turned into a translucent forest
Whose every leaf is speaking fragrant words.

You are familiar with this world; my heart is an extreme white.
After twenty miles of streets I can harvest your steps
That little little
White flower, a little white flower, a little white flower.

崑
南

QUANAN SHUM (SHEN KUN-NAN), 1934–.

b.   Hong Kong.

Founder of the *Modern Literature & Art Association* (with Yip Wai-lim and the painter Wucius Wong), and editor of its publications; now publishes the *Youth Weekly* in Hong Kong.

No statement.

Note: These poems are Quanan Shum's own English translations.

Quanan Shum

THE CONFINEMENT

In a huge room the air of flies fluttering
Youyou babelike looking up the cross window
Between clouds many records and many gods
Youyou spitting a bitter old folk song

Youyou knew well muscles of the stone
Upon which wounded equations and portraits
And signs of astronomy—the moon dripping in
Youyou vented the love juice at the dry bread

On Sunday, a body of snakesmell rattling in
Youyou feigned—the saliva as nightmare bees
Who unlocked youyour days in the chest
When youyou lost in the totem of the three lives

Rockets, computers and all isms, indifferent
Springsummerautumnwinter, same, eyes opened
Stars like ores, ores ballpointing at youyour forehead
Were thrown out with a harvest-gathering heart

Life
Eld
Disease
Death
Youyou and us and them and mankind
Away from the universe
Upon walking
A tortoise
And a snail
The carapace within
Auguring and spiraling
Spiraling and auguring
The carapace within
And a snail
A tortoise
Upon walking

Away from the universe
Mankind and them and us and youyou
Death
Disease
Eld
Life

By the fishbone platter with rats youyou worked
And recalled the matter of hopes and of colony
Of lips and of typewriter and of the key to joy
But not foreigners, nations, cartoons   and not etceteras

A good citizen of the safe island, identified youyou
The foolish drama of time and space—
A delivered corpse on the bed lopped at last
And carted to the gloves of a bad surgeon

The old wish, a secret since youyou're guilty found
Since the wheel less than the machine
Out of the mass-gate into the idea-jail
Youyou wanted no canting priest or painted catacomb

Let fate lock youyour door; on fire youyour voice
With a wax feeling youyou kissed the photo of wife-and-son
After a moment youyour head dwindled on the ground
A blood sun rising from the horizon of that cold wall

THE LEAVES CUT A MOUNTAIN

The leaves cut a mountain
Till birds drink the sun
That horrifies my palms
Then my hair will run run

Into the tomb packed with straw
No water, no passionate ore
I pray for togetherness
While insects withdraw

From the green soil heaven
From the sweet oil fountain
I need you, my old god
But grant me no consolation

Because the moon brother dies
Because I want three eyes
The moral one lives with books
The normal two talentless cry

(Dear yes yes I hate
Sincerely for a money date)

A YOUNG KITE BETWEEN DECEMBER & JANUARY

I

Someone must know the ladder to a star tree
And one hundred and one hours of babe cheer
You see a bearded boy coming down the chimney
Two pale girls letting those stockings free

Please offer me one honey-fish
Together with your mountain memories
Dear, I return my breasts, years
Where no morningmare
But firefly-lea and elephant-sea

Sing a ski-tone and bring a deer-noon
Do buy a winter of red Christ

Who will send us double pocket snowmen
That with many fate hands
Hold up your birthday pants
And cool down my flame sand

And occidental passion
Crossbred with an oriental beauty
Will grow in high December Alas
You and I transmuted by young eternity

II

In a firecracker hour my sore eyes rise
Into the cotton sky, ah, New Year Day
Granting a big hullo, you say, daring play
Play till silly lucks come and pretty evils away

A thick night of crowd in a shape of morn
Your cheeks like sadness-bones like loneliness-thorns
Come, give me the Karma passport, goodbye to dawn
Goodbye to the city where my pity was born

Our young kite will fly when we find and find
A loin of Spring be beaten by child-wings
And time laughs over us; its teeth singing
The oneness of your yearning and my merrymaking

The winter-made flower fair is your pillow dream
I forget the mother-made family and your hot ice cream
No more sick Eve and no more sixteen prince
Dear dear I hate you for your hollow so so clean

AND SPROUT MY LIFE IN WHITE

frequently think of whirling mornings
of hanging suns marked on the musk cloth

when the daffodils stir a day's shape
am cleaning the colors of landscape

turn and you stand against the dream
like a pure tree stretching its green
you laugh to move the wise town
with waves the wind sings of your nouns

in the balcony stays a sky
the electric lines run beautifully around
beyond the hill cloudshadows gather stories
in a sunshine of gulls with sweet south

the full sail be our pink hope
and your eyes the image of last night
'll touch you again in a bath of noon
and sprout my life in white

LO MEN (HAN JEN-CH'UN), 1928–.

b. Kwangtung Province.

Technician in the Civil Air Transport Airline, Taipei.

Poetry: *Aurora* (1958)
          Undercurrent of the Ninth Day (1963)

Statement:

When Man lives with the Ideal, they lie to each other; when Man lives with God, they both become gibberish; when Man returns to himself as man, he is lonelier than anything else.

————from "The Tragic Mind of the Modern Man."

They (the modern poets) are untiring in their devotion to the liberation of the *self,* and are much less responsible for the traditional concepts of reason and morality. At this moment, between man and the self, there is no room left for anybody; not even God or his angels are given the right to sit in. Man does not hope to live in beautiful assumptions and lies; man, living, is eager to embrace the *truth* even if it . . . leads to darkness.

————from "The Spiritual Movement of the Modern Poet"

UNDERCURRENT OF THE NINTH DAY
(Selections)

I

The diamond needle draws a spiral tower of abstract beauty
To prevent buildings from passing away one after the other
The spiral tower immersed in the sun-sea, a miracle dazzling to the
      eyes
Loftiness leads with infinite blue, an icon rises
Roundness and simplicity are busy portraying beauty
Through the crystal windows, sights properly qualified are displayed
When eternity is smashed beneath the corridor of the city
Shreds of time and space attack Miro's vision with complex light
The world is then startled to find itself embarrassed before a
      mirror
And in your tower-kingdom buoyant with sounds and colors
Pure time is being clutched at by the clock's two hands
All things return to their positions, facing one another with still
      the same lovely countenance
My mood is as beautiful as an elegant tablecloth, laid in your
      transparence
Dumb like a snow scene glittering in the moving light of winter

III

Eyes are wounded by the shots of distant mistiness
Days go to see year's face in the speed of seconds
Gardens stop pedestrians with its luxuriance overflowing from the walls
In sombre winter the Christmas flowers are torches held up to the
      Heavenly Kingdom
People preserve a good myth on a card
The hunting cart chased by a snow-storm night
Finally smashes the town's lights. And on the Sabbath Day
Windows are open like the cover of a story book
In your number nine house shaped like a cathedral
The fireplace is fully aflame—the contents are already quite
      warmly baked

Nothing will again copy the unrest of the river
The iron rings, hunting rifles and sticks covering the walls
On the holy Sunday join the chorus
With quiet and harmonious air

IV

Always frightened at the abrupt corner of the corridor
With the gestures of the lamps toward the night, you calm my sight
Two cars pass each other at great speed at the crossroads of my
      heart
Fear and excitement quarrel in whispers—when I am still alive
When the sunshine passes over cold streets to see a gardenful of fallen
      leaves
I am being scrutinized by a date long dead on the calendar
When the two doors of yesterday and tomorrow are slid to the sides
In the wide void, all arms are busy in a kind of reaching out
"Now" still tries to earn people's praises by behaving like a
      flower arranged
Repeated losses are like square bricks piling up into the House of
      Death
Through the terrace and the quiet passage come to the bustling hall
Pour on the red church carpet with satisfaction from the bride's
      bright eyesight
Your musical notes on the ninth day are the eyes of Santa Maria
Regulating the steps that are moving in

IX

For a whole day my island is being fashioned into a relief by
      voiceless waves
A primitive emotion with no language and contemplation of mountains
In a lovely windless season the voyage lies in the folded sail of
      hair
My distant gaze is the sea of distant seas, the sky beyond sky
Very deep when looking down, very high when looking up
I drive a million-mile car on a roadless road, ruts buried in snow

My hands are forced to cross each other before my breast like the
  bolts of the church door
My island is quietly passing the Sabbath Day as leisurely as the
  gardens after harvesting
In a mirror, no more city of clamors, no more market of lanterns
Both stars and moons are tired out in running. Whose boots can
  extinguish the sun?
The horizon is eternally deaf and dumb
When the moving light of evening can no longer flow back to morning's
  East
My eyes get dark on the last axletree
Listening to the sounds of cars moving near, moving afar, moving afar

THE DEATH OF THE CITY
(Selections)

II

Gradations of buildings support the upward gaze of the people
Ranks of food raise waves along their gastric walls
Windows glitter with the bright eyesight of the season
People pick noble looks of the years with bank notes
Here, feet do not transport the soul, nor do they form aesthetics
  from kicking
Here, God is dead; fathers fall into sleep behind the Bible
    All forbidden areas become bustling market places
    All eyes become the eagle-gaze of the blue sky
As cars speed on by pouncing upon the broad open road
People hurry on by clutching at their sail-shaped shadows blown to
  all directions
    To see, within the changes that defy seeing in time
    To think, within the whirls that defy thinking in time
    To die, within the moments that defy dying in time
Speed controls the routes of all organs. God grasps at no phone
It is a busy season, in the intertwining motions

O City! the net you wove is so dense that breathing becomes still
In the stations' anxiety, having been calling to trips
In the tires' tiredness, having been pregnant with distances
And resistance totally canceled, everything slides down the slope
     Rushing toward the last stop
          Falling into the valley of silence
Nobody knows when the sun is going to die
People crouch on piles and piles of negatives
     Failing to call themselves out
     Or to tell the scenery flying in sight
There is nothing that does not go back to the wind
     Just like banquets abscond in a piece of wiping cloth
     Just like vacation dies beneath the still tires

IV

Deep stare into the stirring pool
Flickering shadows form no form
Anxiously smash a mirror—no objects can be extracted
City, in your very unsteady reflection
     All doorknobs and handles are broken
     Some sounds always flit through cracked glass pieces
People hurriedly sow cigarette ends—retrieve themselves from ceilings
To pursue spring   The flower season is over
To view tides   Winds and waves stop
Life is last year's snow   The fallen petals in a puff-box
Death sits on the old sun's sedan
     Calling silently voiced and unvoiced things
     Calling quietly wakened and unwakened world
The ticktocking clock gnaws at the calendar on the floral wall
Shreds, like scattered leaves, spread out Death's soft walk
Hands are a strangler, kind and nimble
Punishment seems tenderer than snoring sleep on quilts
People hide themselves the way they pocket their tickets
No growing of yesterday's branches, no sound of winds gone
City, between rock 'n' roll and dim neonlight
     You are the faceless beast, eating life and leaving no wound behind

VI

City, before the last stop's bell rings
All your turning axles break, running out of rail
Death screams not, showing signal lights
You are like the round-eyed death of Death
Death, in food trays, in ash trays
Death under the Eiffel Tower
When the lung-lobes no longer send news to the ear-trumpets
When badges arrange themselves into a piling mountain scene, shrouding
    the blood-mist
Heaven's door is like a rainbow drawn on the sky for viewers
God can no longer grasp the gradients of towering buildings
City, in Easter everything dies faster
And you are the bride just stepping out from the "floral sedan-chair"
    The wedding night of lanterns. Honeymoon brewed with fruit juices.
    A naked animal in the void primitive plain
    A door screen, covering the shadow of a tomb
    An elaborately engraved coffin holding many moving deaths

CH'IN TZU-HAO, 1911–1963.

b.   Szech'uan Province.

Journalist during the Sino-Japanese Incident; founder of the *Blue Stars Poetry Society* (with Yu, Kuang-chung and others).

Poetry: *Poems of the Ocean* (1954)
          The Sunflower (1955)
          The Art Gallery (1962)
          Complete Works (1965)

Statement:

Style is the poet's own voice. He cannot search for it in any of the schools once prevalent in Europe and the United States. He has to write in such a way that the readers can, from the representations of the poems, see the totality of the Chinese national and cultural spirit, and can hear, from the rhythms, the pulses of the Chinese voice. This is creativity, creativity of the new self. It is in this that one can truly claim to have achieved one's style. New Chinese poetry can thus be, not only of China, but of the world.

——from "Where goes the new poetry?"

EXISTENCE OF A BOTTLE

The zeal that purifies organs sublimes into spirit and spirit acts
    as it feels
Drawing in the breath and sounds of all beings, turning them into
    rhythm
A liberated, autonomous
Rotund belly

A rotund belly
Looks like sitting or standing
The quiet sitting in Zen. The solemn standing of Buddha
Looks like the back or the front
In the back the abyss, in the front the void
In the back the void, in the front the abyss
Nothing is not in the back, it emerges ignoring everything
Nothing is not in the front, it contemplates on all aspects
Not a flat surface, but a cube
Not a square, but a sphere, illuminating and responding to all
    directions
Circular correspondence, circular visibility
An axis, possessing gravity and projection of light
A rotund belly
Waking in slumber, slumbering in waking
Motion in stillness of the self, the unmoved unquiet of the selfless
Existing in the positive as well as in the negative

Not an icon, no eyes nor brows
Not a god, no catechism
An existence, a still existence, an existence of beauty
Formed from images, visible, sensible but indefinite images
The existence of another world
The composite order of the classical, the symbolic
The cubist, the surreal and the abstract
The order of a dream
Born in the spontaneous design of the creator
Emerging in configurations, chaotic but clear, abstract yet concrete
Existing in the nakedness and clarity of thought

Ch'in Tzu-hao

Doze: seven days, Wake: a thousand years
Doze: a thousand years, gathering meditation of a million years
Transform disorder into illumination, clarity into mistiness
Stars and the sun in the cosmic atmosphere
Elegant, uncontaminated as ancient times
Brightening, refreshing as ancient times
So is its stillness, so is its transparence, so is its entire accord
Every inch is light
Every inch is beauty
No need to borrow
No need to decorate

Constellations are majestic
Glittering at night, hidden in the day
The day when not one thing exists
The sun, its master
The blue sky, distant and deep
Conceiving inexhaustible plenitude
The spiritual emptiness in your belly
Is the inexhaustible void

The metamorphosis of a chrysalis, the exuberant blooming and drooping
Butterflies stir their wings, sunflowers sow their seeds
Evolution, succession, and endless cycles?
Or the bursting and subsiding of laughters, in an instant?
Instant after instant
Sunrise, sunset, change of time and time remains unchanged
You are holding the whole of time
Holding a cosmos of loneliness
In the eternal stillness, breathing in and out the void
Self-possessed, liberated and autonomous as the One
And it stills down in the One
And the One remains in the change of solitude
Undissectable
Imperishable

The stillness after complete awakening
The existence after becoming all conscious

The liberated, autonomous
Rotund belly
The cosmos contains you
But your belly conceives another cosmos
And because of you the cosmos exists

GOLDEN MASK

Pupils are invisible, yet the eyesight is profound
                    the elated countenance brightens
See! cold and majestic is the affectionate spirit, when eyelids slightly close
            Is it a silent attraction?
            Is it a relentless challenge?

Eternally staring at the green sea beyond the gallery
Listening to the infatuated song of the sea, praising the abstruse world
            The sea opens one big eye
Casting seven-colored light whirling upon the gallery
Illuminating the anger of your face in your escape from involvements

To the gallery you leave quietude and mystery
How can I look into you inner void?
There is a sensation, like the palm of a hand caressing bushes of flames
        No flesh or skin gets burnt, like the corals
                Burning deep in the green of the sea
A sensation reaches the will
                Like the crane's peck upon gold and stone, clangoring

            Night deepens
            Strings break
In the moment when the candle flames die, you cast a majestic look
        The eyesight becomes two cobras
                With dark glittering
                dark trembling

Skulking out from the cave, rushing to the underworld
        Your eyesight still profound
        Your elated countenance still brightens

How can those Longan eyes be compared to your profundity
Your profound eyes pregnant with insatiable nameless desires
Like me, with fire lurking inside my heart, burning, burning
How to satisfy? Beauty gives me the feeling of the heart
                the ecstasy of organs

The sunflower blooms, petal by petal
    and droops, petal by petal
See! On your face there is extreme heat rising
Yet how is it that it also floats with cold laughs of bronze
Are you looking down upon me?
      Living so happily, so painfully, so peculiarly
Say that you come from Africa, from the Ivory Coast
      On your head are planted red feathers
      On your face are stains of goat's blood-smell
And yet your eyebrows carry such easy gestures
Maybe you come from the ancient opera house of Italy?
O Dream's guide
      Free as you, mysterious as you, distinguished as you
            You I worship
Cupid bribes the God of Silence with a rose
I devote to you with its fragrance
      Please lead me to the dreamland of the future
Not with drum-rattles as rhythm, but with the cadence of the infatuated
    song
In this century, this season
      Only you can make me forget myself
        So as to know the true face of the world

紀弦

CHI HSIEN (LU YÜ), 1913–.

b.   Shensi Province.

High school teacher; editor of *Modern Poetry* (1953–), the first widely influential poetry magazine in Taiwan. ". . . tall like a betel palm; always carries a stick along; his pipe is part of his body; famous drunkard: when drunk, a deluge of tears . . . it is agreed that he is the warmest person in existence."

Poetry: *The Star-Plucking Youth* (1942)
        Drinker (1948)
        The Betel-nut Tree (1965)

Statement:
See all his poems following.

Chi Hsien

COLDNESS

Merely to make me boil up,
She becomes this cold: the air around me.

Air,
With her coldness,
Embraces me.

O Thanks, because
I am this sober
—What I called coldness.
Compared to coldness, especially soberer
There I am; and especially soberer
Compared to me, la
Poésie で あ る.

That is why I boil up constantly,
Sublimating like steam,
And then freeze and congeal into an embraceable solid object.

S'EN ALLER

Heavily beat cacophony upon your piano
And beat with fists like hammers
Beat! Musicians

First headline of the 20th century may be:
12 Yanks first with life visas to moon.
Next, immigration of Japs to Mars
On UN agenda: heated debate.

But my Paris,
(How fragrant!) On which kind
Of earth you do your toe dance?

je m'en vais
tu t'en vas
il, elle s'en va
nous nous en allons
vous vous en allez
ils, elles s'en vont

Besides s'en aller
Also faire, partir, vouloir, etc.
These are irregular verbs
                                    hence beautiful

DEATH OF APHRODITE

Press the Greek goddess Aphrodite into a cow-cutting machine
                    And cut her
                    Into chunks
And abstract all the components
Of BEAUTY
And make them into specimens: then
                                    one small bottle
                                    another small bottle
Classified and specified, displayed in the Museum for Ancient Monuments
        for the public to admire
And be educated.

This is the 20th century: ours.

PROJECTION (1947)

Where I am:
Cigarette ash flying all over.
This:
        The tree of life shedding petals.

And my slender, -er, -est projection stretches beyond the horizon and
        beyond and beyond.

Chi Hsien

EXISTENTIALISM

Like a design
Like a specimen
            a lizard
Night after night, as if dated beforehand
Appears, as if dated beforehand

When I, for tomorrow's bread and
        for yesterday's debt, toil myself,
                working,

Pressing hard on the frosted glass of my window
Over there, using its translucent
Body, its miraculous and ugly-looking
Tail and a head that gives one a creeping feeling
And with the style of our little kindergarten friends' figure paintings
Its four limbs pressing hard,
              like a design
              like a specimen
                  a lizard
This is enough for me to appreciate.
Under the elegant light
Of my lamp: this existence

            This little gecko (made by God)
            This little salamander (made by God)
            A hugh ancient reptile's epitome, abbreviation
                      and clansman
Hushed on the frosted glass of my window
Over there; at times performs food-preying
Stunts; many mosquitoes, moths, green worms
Inside its swelling, virescent stomach are
Being digested
And digested

O yes I am its play-
Goer who applaud for

Its art, with a poem as proof;
And it never pretends not to know,
In this compound of various families and lives,
Who the last one is to turn off the light for bed.

Therefore, I exist—same value as God
The lizard exists—same value as God
Everything exists—same value as God
And this is our existentialism, *our* existentialism

方思

FANG SSU (HUANG SHIH-SHU), 1928–.

b.   Shanghai.

Director of Libraries, Fairleigh Dickinson University—Teaneck Campus.

Poetry: *Time* (1954)
         Night (1955)
         The Harp and the Flute (1959)

Statement:
See the poem immediately following.

FOR A COUNTRY GIRL

Upon the bank, some nameless white flowers.
Water flows to we don't know where.
You pluck rice plants that know no use.
You work
And know not what life is.
Life, to you, is not meaning.

Boats packed with lake mud
Go toward gulfs.
You don't know
Children pick shells on beaches
To compete with the glow of pearls and sunsets.
You don't know
You have lived seriously,
Spring is with you.
Deep green fields.
Deep green water.
Deep green ripeness, fertile.
You, with ease, stand there.
Your life is the deep green.
You are content with your life.

Time stops: no traces,
Although you shake off dews from leaves' backs and
Stop the red glow on wings of returning crows.
Your eyes glitter with brightness.
You never turn a leaf to learn men's history
Or ask about relations among things.
O how vastly deep, this stretch of stillness,
Like a sudden peace:
Such sweetness moistening the soul.
This is a song
Ever bright, ever fresh.
This is life: why do we need art?

Fang Ssu

GROWTH

Look! A tree grows in my heart, in my body.
See how it grows, thrives, though not bathed by
Any warm sun, nor moistened by rains and dews.
Look! It stretches its branches, the way your slender body
Flashes with green leaves, the way you smile as you look back,
The way you, warm and soft, lean upon my heart, my body.

O let pain root, grow, like a tree.
Let it bloom, white like your cheeks; let it fruit,
Smooth like your skin. O let pain grow
In my heart, my body, like a tree, pressing hard upon my heart, my body.
You can caress, with your soft hand, the way you reach into my sleeves;
You can smell its breath with your moistened lips . . . .

Ai, only then can I feel pain, can I
Get used to pain, this deep heart-gouging, skin-rending pain
When the tree presses hard upon me, my body grows: because
                I am the pain itself.

NIGHT SONG

Night eagerly falls down.
Please don't sing dirges.

You have only one form,
But numerous shadows.
Night wrinkles mountains' skirts, stretches trees' arms,
Dissolves water and mist, flattens lakes and dunes.
Night falls down. So,
Tonight's stillness, night's profundity; when sound rises
From the center of silence, there will be light, no shadows:
Your form will be my heart.

Let night fall down prematurely.
I don't want to see you again; your shadows,
Present everywhere, all the time make me lament.
I want to embrace you, merge with you.
My heart embraces you,
Embracing this profound silence, this sonority;
My full heart's, O, silent, happy, life's own sound,
When night falls down, overwhelming the lofty, the low, the distant,
        the near.

Beyond dark, dark; silence, silence.
Beyond.
Please don't sing dirges.

VARIATION OF NIGHT
(A variation by Fang Hsin of a Fang Ssu poem)

O. night
       night eagerly falls down
       please don't sing dirges
       don't catch me with melancholy
       don't try me with suspicious eyes
     I have done nothing but sighing
nothing but sighing   but sighing over this little poverty.
        but sighing over this little poverty.

    december. O. night
on the tropic of cancer   don't catch me with melancholy
a person trails with a black hood   I have done nothing but sighing
   through a white arch   nothing but sighing
   to attend rites for sun's burial   night.   the sun has gone home.
night.   night.   O.   the sun has gone home.

the sun has a home, but I do not.   night.   poverty. little poverty
   night. I even don't know homeland   catch me with melancholy. night
   night.   strange.   night. try me with suspicious eyes
concerning forefathers   nothing but sighing. s-i-g-h-ing. sighing

night.	respectable.	O. little poverty. eagerly.
and I don't know them	night. poverty. poverty.
and upon the glow-watch	eagerly.	night.	falls
a continuous clash	falls. night.	falls down
beginning from prayers in Galilee	night. eagerly. falls down.	this
stole numbers not belonging to me	eager night. falls down	night
and forced their stains	night. eagerly eagerly falls down.
night.	upon my overcoat.

(every	time)
night spreads in darkness	no. don't	songs.
I foot on the fourth string	night.	don't sing
sky. falls rain:	songs	lamenting
	stars weep	lamenting.	songs.
streets are	night.	night.
	long. no shadows	don't sing	songs.
night.	shadows embracing me	songs.	lamenting
	night.	and a half-strolling earth.
		night.	in groups.
		and in groups.	night.	songs.
			night. all names recede
	stars.	night.	don't sing lamenting songs	songs.
	night. million intervals of light-years	receding
	night.	all with names recede. calling another group.
		night. another group. another group. calling another group.
		nobody remembers my name	it's true.	one
				night. and myself	piece
		that is but a piece of lost	of
			night.	lost overcoat	lost
		I am poor	.	over-
			night. even no memory	coat.
			postcards from penguins	.
			night.	cracking beneath icecaps. . . .	.

	. . . tides recede	night
inside distant isles	.
	an only sound	night
	narrating a plotless story	.

harkening   night
  stars all rise   .
I find there is nothing   night
          but an illusion   .
          is but void narrating void.

  night thrives in darkness   night.   night
night.   piling up many-angled bubbles   night.   .
night.   I lie down under a covered nest   night   .night
  night.   fusion hatches me with cool sleepiness   night
    night.   caresses me with Great Bear's velvety tactility   night
    night.   prokofiev flashes by on a tailless comet   .
    night.   I smell magnetic music of an octopus star-cloud   night
      night   from a transistor channel, indifferent sneering   night.
    night.   sneering my brewing of joy   night
night.   night night.   joy   joy   but I don't have.

      I don't even dare expect anything.
      dare not   before daybreak's advent
      songs.   escape from whirlpool cosmos
      to say anything   no   dare   not
      not even this little poverty   . night
      O. night.   would also be lost.

HSIN YÜ (FU SHIH-SHEN), 1933–.

b.　Checkiang Province.

Former soldier, publisher, columnist.

Poetry: *Notes by a Sergeant* (1961)

Statement:

Modern poetry no longer aims at reflecting the external aspects of the objects or chanting over the phenomenal world. "Reflection" can no longer grasp the instantaneous change of the inward vision and spirit. The true countenance of the hidden objects cannot be brought to light except through new expressions . . . .

COMING TO THE SEA
(Four Poems)

I

People have not yet gathered, ferryboat

Dusk has not mantled the summit, ferryboat

Wine-flags are still fluttering—it's high time for drinking
Ferryboat

Girls are eating vegetarian food at the monastery
The ban-lifting bell is reposing
Ferryboat

But the boatman has come already
Although he has come . . . .

II

On my seaweed-smelling bosom
Charged with fishy dampness, a ferryboat
Is at a tacet

O! When will the music be played?

A man on the bank plants some poles
Tightens the cordage and leaves

The sun shines on the dike and on the boat
In an afternoon in June

III

The pregnant girl comes again
Lost fishingboats quietly
Quietly now entering into Time's cycle

And connecting the boiling life
The horizon stretches its long long
Immanent arms

The pregnant girl comes again
In the evening. At an arm's length
A gray tract of wall stops the way

And connecting the boiling life
The horizon stretches its long long
Immanent arms

IV

Noises of machinery
Temptation of heaped-up phosphorescence

Imagine a merciless slap on the faces
Of indulgent gamblers spending a whole night at a table
(Who look pale, pregnant with regrets)
Grumbling over their bad luck to their wives

But no one understands why this
Flaming ball kindled
By lustful eyes, comes and goes
Turning speedily

Maybe, dignity is at your feet
Because you, losing your mask
Carelessly, and carelessly again
Cast away the garment of your eyes' language

But I have been angry
For no end
Just like a dull cat
Walking over an empty food tray

But are we
Stranded at all

Each in his own location—without losing the sea-book
Without becoming two ships
Whose mainmasts are broken?
It seems that no one would come to untie the cordage
In an afternoon
In a chord of sky apportioned to me
My entirety seeks
Some kind of requiem
                    and what about you?

I want to confirm if you, too, were
Fascinated by the scenery at the border
And shed tears which become, you said, the sowing of seeds.

EPITAPH: SEVEN LINES

This man who did not like inscriptions was
Drowned in the flirting eyes of autumn's bereaved woman

A species in the bushveld
He treasured in his last
Conception a non-verbal
Grief for the mundane
Besides which, nothing else was left behind

MOTHER, MOTHER

A crystal moon is rising:
Such soft footsteps!
Mother, mother
My dream of flight glides down: there, autumn dew,
Ice-cold sorrow in earth's bosom,
A flow of all images rush

Toward me—I look for anchoring or rest,
Just as a coffin looks for some rotten smell.
I am unpurged   un-
Soaked by the denuding liquid.

Winds blow and shine upon my growth.
The sun stains me with the color of soil.
But city! On a perilous tower, where can I go?
What can I follow? How can I, peeping into a bottle,
See big boots, by contrast, tread upon my gray forehead.

These are your drums and cymbals, your salt-smelling riches,
Old Sky! These are the victuals in your barn;
These are even an immense empire.
Upon the square, a flight of wings drift.
A set of silverware enters your heart's center.

Because of this, I think of the day when you closed your eyes forever,
Mother, mother
The nectar that you never got to brew drips, winging into the sky.
The high-spirited limping song raising many flags,
I know my heart's majestic kingdom has crumbled.

Now to convey thus with hand gestures,
To believe the cloud-sky is truly lofty.
In this moment, I wish I were a little purple flower
Of pure species waiting to be appreciated.
Lifting my head, I cry out silently: Mother, mother.

O PLAINS
(Words from a brother in Mainland China)

Are you the fragrant plains which my arms, stretching, can reach and where
    the air brims wild?
Are you the plains which become my clothes in the day, my blankets at
    night, which bathe living forms and nourish living forms?

You make the sorghum grow tall;
You fatten all the beans;
You strengthen deers' hooves;
You, plains,
You are a clear fountain in my pupils; you cleanse the dust of my years;
You are the most revered, most handsome god I worship,
O
You are life's infinity, infinitely extending, most sacred and goodly.

    What are sunflowers?
You said:
    Sunflowers are poems written on my skin by the sun.

    What about chrysanthemums?
You said:
    Chrysanthemums are the Orient's pride.

O Orient, Orient,
    Where are my yellow-skinned brothers?
    Where are my yellow-skinned brothers?
    (Outside the dungeon, have you worshipped, with the devotion due
    a god, the most revered, most handsome, most sacred and goodly
    plains the way I worship them?)
  Brothers,
O brothers,
Please listen to my chewing of the iron bars.
Please see how I stare at the dark, dark curtain.
Please sing to me.
    (How I hunger to hear the flowing, southwindlike songs!)
Please sing,
Sing with your guns,
Brothers,
This is time for you to sing with your guns.

One day,
Tempests bit off my eyelashes.
Since then, my eyes could not open for light;

My ears could not grow for sound.
Since then, they
Pickled all the orioles' tongues, pickled spring thunders, pickled stars,
Pickled the sun and me; since then,
In the pickled days I chewed,
O plains,
Do you know what is it that I chewed?
The brine of decomposed life,
This smelling brine I chewed.
My brothers,
My yellow-skinned brothers,
Did you hear my teeth crack, my tongue break?

Embrace
    with this left-over life
Embrace
    with heart dripping blood
Embrace, embrace
   dream
   embracing
O plains
I embrace your shadows.

KUAN KUAN (KUAN YÜN-LUNG), 1929–.

b.   Shantung Province.

Engineer in the Armed Forces (Broadcasting Division).

Statement:

In my opinion, the poet never intends any "meaning" in a poem. If there is a meaning, it will be the fearful (to me, beautiful) truth. Poetry demands nothing. It is of itself; it is of art. If the word "meaning" is what is sometimes called "biblical aphorisms," I hate it. I do not want to offer the readers any pattern for living. This is a fraud. One should rely on nothing except himself for his own existence, or on a god he wilfully chooses, not Jesus nor Confucius, but himself.

Writing poetry is my living god. It is at the same time a play, a most voluntary play—it is, in one sense, a selfish kind of action. But whom can I save? Poetry gives me a delight; except this, there is nothing. Do you not see that, although there are many bibles, we are still so impatient?

THE MAN WHO RUBBED HIS FACE WITH FIREFLIES

A pack of bitches were biting the sea and the evening.
Eight o'clock sharp. The man who had just taken over the sentry saw with his own eyes the evening's red-embroidered shoes being stolen and the sea's skirt torn to pieces by bitches.—O what a strange man!—he did not even fire his rifle at them or report this to the lieutenant, but became absorbed in the beauty of a wild chrysanthemum he planted in his barrel and insisted that it was a woman; and then, he hummed a happy tune: *Little mother, I am brave and brassy.*

'Signal fires continue for three long months;
A letter from home is worth a thousand pieces of gold.'

But he did not know that without shoes, evening could not return home, that the sea lay on the beach among torn pieces of skirt, weeping. A bitch was mouthing a flare bomb she believed to be a fallen sun; he ought to have believed it, too. But this man, ugh! I simply cannot bear the sight of him.

A shot from the gun gave the night eyes to see. Meanwhile the night was herding a gang of mice and the moon was herding a school of flying fish. This man grasped a handful of fireflies and rubbed his face with them, saying that his face was hung with stars. He held up his rifle and desperately shot at the stars. Because the mice had eaten away the stock of his rifle? Or maybe because the Hunter had come down to steal his rabbit and had eaten it up and had drunk his *kao-liang?*[1] But the lieutenant said these were no reasons. It was simply that the lieutenant disliked the sight of him. The next day he would go to buy a ticket and drink wine.

A STOPOVER VISITOR

1

1. Buds cry out with wide mouths. What are they crying out for? Spring stays at the tips of sister's long pigtails. Little swallows cannot find the house

---

[1] *Kao-liang* is a strong spirit made from sorghum.

numbers of now. The fingernails of the grass sprain embroidered shoes in a spring excursion.
Believe it or not, a butterfly, passing, treads on my shoulder.

2

2. I see you in a fan. At night, I knock down stars with a bamboo stick the way autumn knocks down persimmons from trees. Night is laden with eyes, frog-eyes. It is so hot. Why doesn't earth jump down to take a bath? The neck of a sunflower is scarfed with a rainbow.

3

3. In the forest
Fruits and fruits clamor noisily, nagging the wind, complaining that he should not, really should not have cut their slips into such a beautiful confusion and let pass the shoes of a young man whose collars are turned up.
And who is at the same time smoking.

4

4. I tidy up spring, summer and autumn like a pack of paper money and burn them in a chafing pan. I burn one sheet, I cry once; I cry once, I burn one sheet. This sickness! The firecrackers will speak to you and I will have to ride on an ass to announce the death from house to house.
"Floating scents mixing in moonlit dusk"

MY YOUNGER BROTHER'S KINGDOM

1

(A young soldier in a raincoat is reading sheets of epitaphs)

My younger brother beautifies my annual rings one by one and flips them

Note: Chafing pan in China reminds one of the funeral rite of burning paper money for the dead. "Floating . . . dusk" is a quotation from Lin P'u, a Sung poet.

at me again and again with his glass eyeballs, flipping out some cruel stories of youth, flipping out some green and bitter stars. Stars.

(Outside the city. Spring. The petals of pear flowers, like pages and pages of funeral odes, drift with the wind, across circles and circles of beautiful ripples, drifting with such homesickness.)

Ah! Tai-yü, the frail beauty! Tai-yü!
      Eastward flows the Yangtze River! Scouring heroes and worthies of
          all times!

(Your moss-grown face, covered with deep lines like scripts on oracle bones, and heavily knotted with ropes—a face my younger brother simply does not care for.) A top-shaped face is being whipped and whipped . . . drifting and drifting like the strokes of Yen Chen-ch'ing's calligraphy. You are a kite whose line is broken, drifting and drifting with such homesickness!

(Your face is pasted all over with newspapers, official notices, with restless ants crawling here and there.)
My younger brother builds a round city with iron rings; he does not allow you to get in and your beard, to him, is worthy of nothing but sweeping the floor.
(A young soldier in a raincoat is reading tablets of epitaphs)

2

May I ask if the soft feather-fan between your eyes
Could drive away the dry leaves that covered my face?

ONE SPRING MORNING IN A TOWN CALLED YM

It took only two dogs to clean up the street
For a fish-bone, merely for a fish-bone, the dogs in no time
Bit the smooth street into many boils,
      And made the peach blossoms, sick near garbage cans (How slim
      they were!), look more haggard.

The sun in town was always the most industrious.
He always grasped, from clothes hanging on terraces,
Handfuls of clouds and planted them wherever he pleased,
    And, in this way, tempted chimneys to foster a smoking habit,
    Issuing lone smoke-pillars on the wilderness.

The town's eyes, reflecting convulsions of every description, were
    still closed, its ears cocked to listen to horse hooves, the
    ringing of the most solitary of all hanging chimes, and to the
    sun riding on a monocycle past the camel humps of the green-tile
    houses, rumbling
When the white-headed man spit his first rather musical phlegm, and
    afterwards?

Suddenly a military truck in a hurry-scurry passes
When we are reminded of the clashes of arms in the camps on the distant
    hills
When we are reminded of, reminded of what?
Or else, the townspeople would be living stolidly inside the mildewed
    paintings on the east wall of the herb drugstore?
In the village, the peach blossoms at the well next to the secret whorehouse
    grin and grin.
Some soldiers, in spite of everything, break the budding flowers like mad,
    scattering them onto a brimming fountain.

ROSE AND WINTER

At the port, I pluck down cannon shells from the rim of my helmet. (Go, go
    back to your blue front. I hope you are a mackerel.) Don't worry. I am
    not the man who throws the net. These disturbing, barren years.

Who doesn't adorn himself with a gun these days? Whose helmet doesn't
    carry a silver-bright dagger at its rim?
    (Oh! I have no fish. I have no fish. I have no fish.)

Don't you see our "brothers" write their diaries with bullets, scrabbling them

upon white iron-sheets? How particular! One brother wrote only the word LOVE　愛　, which looks like the seedcase of a lotus. So many empty eyes. Through the seedcase, a rifle range (Violent thuddings of guns); a green prairie (The wind blows, the grass bends, the cattle are visible); a quiet river (Eastward flows the Yangtze!) sugar-cane fields (My younger brother's private kingdom); chimneys (The sun's pipes); the sea (The homeland of blueness, the graveyard of the fish); the azure (The heaven of kites, the pasture of stars); and there is the frisky sun.
Who doesn't adorn himself with a gun these days? Who doesn't become a tortoise hurrying on its way?
(Oh! I love beasts　　I love beasts　　I love beasts)

Don't take off your uniform. He is one of our brothers. Let me also read the rattling of drums that is found with you—How beautiful, this rattling! You are not my first man. You come from the rattling and will return to the rattling. You are my man who loves wine and women, and is head-strong in these matters all the time.

When I think of the black shields and the white teeth of these boys, I should say that the words of our district prefect are just too true.

If one sees a turtledove flying overhead, he who doesn't raise his gun (Damned him who doesn't!) is not high-class at all. Whose "nest" is not built on the road? Go, and there will be scenery and scenery and scenery
A driving whip: the afterglow
Four sides, the light of mountains
Winter (that old witch with an arid face) leaves me nothing but the rose-color of a young girl—the color of a rose of a young girl, that will be enough, the color of a rose of a young girl.

"A rare sword inside the scabbard. Sound of night."

A LITTLE GIRL

Night after night a little girl with flying long hair standing upon a plank balcony raised her small face toward the sky.

It was that day: Everybody saw it. I saw it.
    Every star stretched a small hand,
    Every small hand clutched a hair,
So quietly, no one is disturbed, they took her away.

SPRING SONG

Spinning the whole night, still undone, spinning mist on an apricot tree,
This sister (why, nothing at odds with her) is spinning weeping.

Three or four snakes wiggle, shaking off all the dirt,
Wiggling—up to a phoenix fern beneath the wall and
Open—wide mouths (O heck!) to sun themselves under the breathless sun.
Are the two kites flying two children or the two children flying two kites?
Another one, neckstretched, is watching kites (O his mother's . . . !) flying
        a skyful;
And a dog on the wheat field is biting a kite.
All the birds stretch their throats, stretch until (O his mother's . . . !) they
        become a long trumpet
             and blow to front streets & to back streets
             and blow to right streets & to left streets
And finally blown up to the ash tree, from which is hanging a swing.

Southeast corner: rows of peartrees; their buds,
Since last night, begin to have their (O delicious!) explosion.
Explosions are explosions; pear flowers are pear flowers
                but they are certainly not strings
Of thuddings—of guns
                nor are they (O his mother's . . . !) the skyful
Of strings—of kites.
A wooden flute distantly whines around a stretch of willow forests by the
        South River.
In each floral sedan chair is always a bride.
Old buddy, you have to admit
    Spring is but an affair at a throw
    And bombs—boom! also an affair at a throw.
Amen. Namo amitābha-buddhāya.